THE CLUE OF THE
RED THREAD

Angélique Kauffmann (1741–1807), Ariadne Giving a Ball of Thread to Theseus

THE CLUE OF THE RED THREAD

discovering fearlessness and compassion in uncertain times

JULIE TALLARD JOHNSON
in collaboration with
Parker J Palmer

and poetry by Rebecca Cecchini

Nine Rivers
Brunswick, Maine

THE CLUE OF THE RED THREAD
Discovering Fearlessness and Compassion in Uncertain Times

Copyright © 2021 Julie Tallard Johnson

All rights reserved. This book or any portion thereof may not be reproduced or used in any manner whatsoever without the express written permission of the publisher except for the use of brief quotations in a book review.

Published by Nine Rivers, an imprint of Shanti Arts Publishing

Cover and interior design by Shanti Arts Designs

Shanti Arts LLC
Brunswick, Maine
www.shantiarts.com

Printed in the United States of America

Cover image is a photograph of a labyrinth carved on a pillar of the portico of Lucca Cathedral in Tuscany, Italy, by Myrabella, 2011. Wikimedia Commons. Creative Commons.

Ruth Ozeki Lounsbury, *A Tale for the Time Being*, Penguin Random House. Copyright 2013. Excerpts used with permission of the publisher.

All names and identities of individuals referred to as students or clients are fictional and the stories connected with them are composite narratives.

ISBN: 978-1-951651-65-7 (softcover)
ISBN: 978-1-951651-66-4 (digital)

Library of Congress Control Number: 2021930114

*Dedicated to Carole K
and all my Al-Anon sisters and brothers*

Maestro di Tavarnelle, sixteenth-century, Theseus and the Minotaur. Louvre Museum, Paris, France.

CONTENTS

– OUR MYTH –
THE LABYRINTH AND THE CLUE OF THE RED THREAD
13

– INVITATION –
HERE, TAKE THIS GIFT
17

TAKING HOLD OF THE RED THREAD:
LIVING LIFE FROM THE INSIDE OUT
21

UNWINDING THE THREAD:
LIVING WITH CONTRADICTIONS
41

BAREFOOT IN THE LABYRINTH: PENETRATING ILLUSION
THROUGH ACTIVE CONTEMPLATION
57

THE LABYRINTH'S AQUIFERS: THE WELL-FED SPIRIT
69

MEETING UP WITH THE MINOTAUR:
FACING AND INTEGRATING SHADOW SELF
83

THE RETURN JOURNEY:
AT THE THRESHOLD OF EXPERIENCE
101

**GATHERING THE THREAD ON THE WAY OUT:
GIVING SHAPE TO THE WORLD
119**

**RETURNING TO THE WORLD:
THE THREAD OF TRUE COMMUNITY
135**

**HANDING OTHERS THE RED THREAD:
LEADERSHIP AS EVERYONE'S VOCATION
153**

**KEEPING HOLD OF THE RED THREAD IN THE WORLD:
THE CLAIM TO AUTHENTIC SELFHOOD
175**

**– A MESSAGE FROM PARKER J. PALMER –
FROM TEACHER TO TEACHER:
OUR RED THREAD LINEAGE
187**

. . .

**ENDNOTES
193**

**BIBLIOGRAPHY
195**

**IN GRATITUDE
199**

**ABOUT THE AUTHOR
ABOUT THE POET
201**

We enter in
shifting, unknown, uncharted, yet to be
determined ways.
Breath we have. Spark and salt, flesh and bone
alive—and that is mostly triumph.

So happens again and again as we go,
the ground surrounding, by some turn, is laid bare
of once familiar forms.
But there is no such thing as traversing alone,
as they say we come, or as they say we leave
(not so those either).

Still, you have to go through
your own disillusionment. I'm sorry for that.
But that's not the test—
it will be something more like:
once through, did you salvage
your child mind?

Can you respond once more with trust or hope,
with generosity or mercy, in your world since—revealed?

A trading of parts, being part, and taking part, is this life.
And you already embody the whole Holy within
revelation. This, and the stars in you, is all true.

For some thread of finest spark, Wisdom spun,
and handed along,
bursts with torch brilliance when held
aloft. Lights the paths of many. Yours too,
who once received. Pass it.
That's all. And when you see
its brighter—yet spinning and higher—yet reaching
in the hands of another and another
after that,
be joyful. Your burden was Light,
your work well done.

OUR MYTH

THE LABYRINTH AND THE CLUE OF THE RED THREAD

Imagine young men and women in your country and neighborhood being routinely sent to war, working in hospitals to deal with a pandemic without safety masks, or confronting such daily horrors as hate crimes, gun violence, and sexual assault. Imagine further that those in power expect their citizens to sacrifice themselves on the altar of the economy, false patriotism, and revenge at a time when guns, money, and autonomy outrank dignity, community, and justice. Imagine further that you choose to act against these injustices to serve your people as best you can and defend humanity and democracy.

In Greek mythology, the king's daughter Ariadne lived in the palace of Knossos on Crete where she was put in charge of its many mazes and labyrinths. Crete was known as a place of "extremes and contradictions."[1] Underneath the Knossos palace was a complex and deadly maze built by the master designer Daedalus to house the Minotaur. Daedalus himself got lost in this maze, almost to die there.

Young men and women from Athens were routinely sent into the maze to be devoured by the Minotaur in a sacrificial rite of revenge. Theseus, an Athenian prince, came to free Athens from its commitment of sacrifice and vowed to enter the maze and kill the Minotaur. Ariadne fell in love with Theseus, and because she loved him, she resolved to come to his aid. She gave Theseus her ball of red thread so he might fasten it to the labyrinth's entrance, then unravel it to mark his passage into its center. When Theseus initially took hold of the ball of red thread, the deadly maze was instantly transformed into a negotiable labyrinth—though still with its challenges and deceptions—which he was then able to enter, confront the Minotaur, and safely return out.[2]

Ariadne's thread was a guiding device. As there was not an easy way to memorize the paths of the labyrinth, the thread helped overcome the difficulties and limitations of memory. Even when someone successfully met up with the Minotaur, they never found their way out and died trapped inside the maze. The ball of thread is known as a *clew* (or clue) to solving the labyrinth, which had countless paths, some of which were treacherous.

Theseus represents that part of us that can be forgetful and too often sacrificed on the platform of someone else's aspirations and plans. He is also the heroic part of us that is altruistically motivated and willing to break agreements with those in authority in order to serve humanity.

Courageous people who have gone before or are beside us now hand us the red thread of their wisdom to help transform us into heroic figures. All teachings and teachers come to us as part of a lineage. The red thread in this book represents the lineage of my teachers' teachings, including that of Parker J. Palmer, handed over to us here as an expression of their and my love.

Because our lives are full of forked paths, contradictory twists and turns, and frequent dead ends, and because we can sometimes forget who we are, we often need a guiding thread, a clue to help us successfully navigate our own particular labyrinths. Taking the thread of teachings gives us the confidence to reach our internal center as well as face our Minotaur, and then safely find our way back home to self, purpose, and community once more. This is what the everyday heroine looks like.

Just as with Theseus in the myth, our assumptions, emotions, memories, and beliefs may be unreliable and thus lead us astray. Ultimately, they become the constructs of our mazes. Other people, too, may try to manipulate us into following their agenda for our lives. Once we firmly take hold of the red thread of teachings, however, we are wholly capable of traversing the many twists and turns in our lives for ourselves. We do not have to be sacrificed to appease anyone, nor do we have to live life lost in a maze constructed by us or someone else.

At each turn in our metaphorical labyrinth (and very real life!), we unravel more of the red thread, revealing some promise and tangible hope contained in each teaching. Each time we place the red thread on the ground to mark a clear path back out, we also "place down" inside of us an understanding and realization that we will continue to carry within us. The thread may unwind and weave as we make our way through the labyrinth of our lives, but it can never break. This red thread, unlike breadcrumbs, will not be devoured by some hungry bird, but remain within us always as lasting nourishment for our souls and communities.

INVITATION

HERE, TAKE THIS GIFT

The soul wants to give us life and wants us to pass that gift along, to become life-givers in a world that deals too much death.

—Parker J. Palmer

Parker J. Palmer's teachings and mine come from a similar dye. Though we have different lineages of teachers, our paths at times have been parallel, for we advocate and teach themes that are similar: living life from the inside out, understanding and developing our true nature, living with contradictions, trusting our inner truth, and being in authentic relationship.

During initial conversations about the possibility of this book (the one you hold in your hand), Parker referred to his core teachings as "red threads."

I trusted the arrival of the red thread as a well-timed metaphor. Through Parker's intuitive nature, the helping spirits, and my own explorations, I chose the red thread as the thematic metaphor for this book. This makes for that perfect blend of an active life that Parker and I so often refer to, one in which we trust what arises out of authentic conversation, we actively engage in contemplative action through our observations, and we acknowledge that there is an underlying filament of Spirit helping bring together what is truly possible.

With each turn we take in the metaphorical labyrinth, which represents particular points in our lives, we use a red thread teaching and related practices offered here to help us explore and try on a particular concept for ourselves. We take hold of the red thread clues to go down into the centers of ourselves, confront our fears and limitations, and come back out to our communities truer to our calling and inner nature.

In exploring these teachings for ourselves, we come to recognize the potential within each of life's turns and circumstances. Life is about holding onto and passing on the red thread, which, of course, is a metaphor for the available wisdom and possibilities present in any given situation. The red thread is a rich analogy for how we can unravel the truth contained within us to navigate our outer life at any point, no matter the circumstances. **As it turns out, the greatest and most needed adventure of our life is to go inward and, ultimately, live from the inside out.**

At the start of each chapter there are sutra-like quotes of Parker's that provide a way to explore and contemplate these and other teachings. There are also verses and poems by Rebecca Cecchini, this book's poet. Her verses are presented at places where you may want to pause and contemplate the teachings and practices offered to you. In my Buddhist practice, I rely on sutras to remind me of the spiritual principles I want to live by and that inspire me to do so. "Sutra" comes from the root word *suture*, which coincidentally translates as "thread." These threads of verse and quotes can transform the internal maze of a confused mind into a ready mind, one receptive to reality. In reading sutras and poems, we relax into the verse and let its words and meaning move through our hearts and minds effortlessly. While continuing to keep hold of the conceptual thread—a given spiritual teaching—our focused mind is able to confront and live with the exterior world of complexities and contradictions without losing contact with our inner truth. As with all good myths and teachings, we are to understand these red thread teachings as clues—clues that lead us to our own unique knowing; clues that lead us all the way into our being and then back out again to enrich our lives and communities; clues that help us trust our personal experiences no matter what is going on around us.

The Clue of the Red Thread

Red thread clues come to you here in quotes, teachings, questions, poems, and practices to explore for yourself. The best teachings only offer clues because in this way we are trusted with discovering their meaning for ourselves. Besides, Parker, as is the case with all great teachers, actively follows a red thread of clues down to his center. In so doing, all authentic teachers are fully activating the spiritual and creative components of their lives. Once we have taken this gift of the red thread, it can continuously be given and received in all our interactions as clues to living our life to the fullest.

In studying Buddhist sutras and other valuable spiritual texts, I have found that the knowledge that is shared within any particular tradition is not consistent. So, in many ways, we are on our own when we attempt to harvest meaning from what various teachings offer us. In our willingness to go into our own knowing, the thread of this book's teachings escorts us to the divine principle of our belonging. For in accepting the red thread, using it as a clue to guide us in our daily life, and then, in our becoming good citizens and leaders, we choose to pass the thread on to others in true fellowship.

I offer this book with its clues and verses as a red thread to you, as an invitation to experience the reciprocity and vastness that life truly offers each of us at every moment, at each turn of life's labyrinth. In so doing, I also gift back all my teachers and their lineage of teachers by being a living expression of their work

**Please Please
come,
find me in the dark.
use your eyes-closed
vision. if you would, come,
with your noiseless flutter, and meet me
in the hollow, there where neither morning nor
night
hold sway
but each seen as part, filled
with,
in that whole of day.**

in the world. Finally, I like to remind my clients and students to "come as you are" to these teachings. Don't feel you have to be anything in particular or reach any certain understanding. My conversations with Parker, as with all the great teachers in my life, were implicitly held with the invitation to come as I am, to be as I am, and to discover for myself.

So, Dear Reader, come as you are, take this gift of the red thread of teachings and clues, and together, again, we can discover what we are truly capable of.

CHAPTER ONE

TAKING HOLD OF THE RED THREAD: LIVING LIFE FROM THE INSIDE OUT

All truly human activity emerges from one's inwardness.

—Parker J. Palmer

Having taken the red thread, we get ready to step into our sacred work and claim (or reclaim) our foothold in the world. *Our first red thread lesson is a fundamental invitation: to live our life from the inside out, which means to consciously relate to every circumstance with some purposefulness and intention and to make claim to our inner lives in a way that brings forth our greatest selves and capacities.*

We make so many decisions each day, most of them affecting countless others. All our decisions and actions are driven by particular emotional and cognitive states and inner narratives such as shame, courage, doubt, trust, fear, jealousy, and possessiveness. Shame, for example, may generate actions that somehow shame others. Fear tends to make us more fearful and susceptible to the authority of others. We want to be conscious of these inner narratives because they have real consequences in our lives and in the lives of others. We want our actions to reflect an awareness that comes from within: a knowing of who we are, what our light and dark aspects are, and what we truly want.

What motivates us? This is a good thing to know. Awareness,

a keen consciousness to our inner life, allows for a safer, saner, and more fulfilling outer experience.

We can start every journey by making claim to our rich inner world, our truest callings and being. This means our gaze and efforts come from the inside and go out, rather than from the outside going in. This means we meet others halfway as we *live life from our side*.[3]

This way of being in the world is often rejected as being self-centered. Yet quite the opposite is true. Living from the inside out, from our side of the conversation, recognizes the fundamental and universal truth that whatever is experienced on the outside is directly related to our inner landscape. Much outside of us tries to claim us. When we tap into our inner life, we can maintain a strong directional pull, but where we are not conscious, we may find ourselves being pushed around by outer circumstances.

When we review our life and recall times when we experienced a positive shift or even an epiphany—either through someone else's guidance or our own experience—we find that what truly changed was some sentiment we held within. Our "aha" moments arrive from internal shifts, not external circumstances. At the core of all relatable teachings is our underlying counsel on how to live life connected to our inner truths and callings.

TAKE YOUR BLIND DOG FOR A WALK

After my first conversation with Parker about this book, I was flooded with gratitude, and I wondered what had brought forth such intensity of emotion. The next day, as I took my blind dog for a walk, I realized exactly where this feeling of persistent peace and deep gratitude came from.

Cookie, our yellow lab, had been blind for a year. I was her "seeing-eye person." On our walks, her pace was fast and straight in front of me, even keeping me walking more quickly than I might otherwise. It was hard to believe she was blind. Her actions contained such certainty, such self-assurance. Her tail wagged as she walked. On our walk that day after speaking with Parker, I watched her go quickly and deliberately in front of me, and I realized she was able to move with confidence because she trusted me—completely. And this trust of hers created walks that were joyful for us both. That was it! Toward the end of my conversation with Parker, he had said, "I trust you completely, Julie." (Though in this version of the story, I am the blind dog. Or, as Parker might say, it is the blind joyfully leading the blind.)

Trust is a potent antidote. We can travel far, perhaps even going ahead of our teachers on our own when those whom we rely on for guidance are trustworthy, and they trust us.

Trust is fundamental if we are to move forward on our spiritual path as well as truly engage with others. Trust is a vulnerability. First, we need to trust ourselves—trust ourselves enough to take the next inward and outward measure—then trust others enough to open ourselves to them. And in our own way, which is compatible with our spiritual bent, we trust our spiritual source. Basically, trust makes movement imaginable. And when we imagine something, it becomes more possible. Every action starts in our imagination. Trust makes it possible to walk forward into the Great Unknown—like a blind, happy dog. We don't know what we will find when we take our next step. We can never be certain of another's response. We don't know—and often don't witness—the outcome of our actions.

When I heard, "I trust you completely," I further understood the nature of trust and the depth of its reward. Being trusted is a profound way to be seen and known. Seeing and knowing someone results from doing our internal work, from living life from the inside out. Such trust, in its expression, is reciprocal and spacious. Otherwise, we tend to withhold in some congested state of distrust. Trust gives us permission to be ourselves, to walk ahead, to explore internal and external possibilities, to risk. Our expressed trust in others opens us and the other to what is truly possible. As Frank Fools Crow states in *Fools Crow: Wisdom and Power*, "Without faith there is no power and there is no movement."

Trust given and received makes us braver and opens both the giver and the receiver to a wider berth of potential. We are more likely to act heroically and take risks when trust is at the foundation of our actions. Finally, you will find, as I did, that trust opens us to the generosity of others and to the presence of Spirit.

Part of our heroic engagement with others is in offering and acknowledging one's trust for another. This happens when instead of focusing on and communicating our anxieties or doubts about another, we internally explore our anxieties while expressing trust to those around us. We don't feel the need to walk ahead and tug at our blind dog, making false assumptions about their capabilities. For me, the trust I have in my young adult daughter as she adventures further into her adulthood can now be as complete and simply conveyed as that demonstrated to me by Parker. Mutual trust gives us sight even in dark times. With an acquaintance, we can rely on and express a trust in our shared humanity and enjoy a willingness to open up to the other. Also, trust can help us let go of past grievances and meet the other with fresh eyes.

Notice, too, where you have an opportunity to convey trust "on the spot" with what or who is before you. You can notice when an inner dynamic such as resistance, expectation, or anxiety arises and take this as an opportunity to invite trust and receptivity. Imagine opening your heart and mind in the moment, letting go of pushing an agenda or pulling away from the encounter. Be curious. *Let the blind dog take the lead.* Put voice to this trust and witness a wider, more generous route opening before you. All movement forward in our lives—all the times we are receptive and open—is an expression of trust. As I walk ahead, sometimes blindly, the tether to my red thread teachings gives me a faithfulness to walk courageously into and with uncertainty. When this happens, the other and I, in our mutual expression of trust, become Spirit made manifest.

> **Listen.**
> **Ten million peepers chime light in the dark**
> **come spring**
> **to map a starry sky for the blind,**
> **and those who can't see.**

THE ATTITUDE OF EXPLORATION

Our personal experience is our best evidence of what works and what does not work. There are many formulas and programs offered up to the hungry seeker that take away the responsibility of exploring and noticing for ourselves. When we rely on such formulas and programs, we live life from the outside in and miss out on the greatest gift life has to offer: discovering truth for ourselves. "When people lose their sense of awe, people turn to religion. When they no longer trust themselves, they begin to depend upon authority" (Lao Tzu, *Tao Te Ching*, as translated by Stephen Mitchell). We can thoroughly celebrate and integrate our personal awareness into our lives. We can come to trust and explore our personal experiences like my blind dog used her nose.

Exploration is curiosity without anxiety. It's important that we explore within the context of our daily lives, meaning we don't need to attend special retreats, pay expensive teachers, or find that guru on the mountain. Our power to awaken to our greatest potential or to transform negativity is here, now. No matter our circumstances, and maybe because of them, we can be heroic, save relationships, create a masterpiece, or generate world peace within our life situations and from the inside out.

> **oh thank you!**—to all the Fools
> **willing to inherit that freehold of territory within,**
> **along with said title,**
> **in exchange for claiming its wide open joy**
> **to believe**
>
> **that fox *did* come by to tell you**
> **something.**

EXPLORING A DYNAMIC

In my year-long Red Thread Circles, each participant, at the start, finds a dynamic to explore. Also, any time in my life when I feel stuck, overwhelmed, or negative, I do this practice to transform negativity on the spot. A dynamic is an inner state that shows up in our lives and perhaps trips us up: blame, fear, jealousy, shame, expectation, co-dependency, self-doubt, competitiveness, isolation, need for instant gratification, or dependence on outer validation—to name a few that are frequently identified. Of course, these inner states also show up in the outer landscape of our lives, but in order to transform our experience, we must first identify this dynamic from within. We explore, for example, how fear originates from within and how we carry it and believe it, and we then witness how it is expressed and how it arises in the outer conditions of our lives. We also discover how outward circumstances trigger our particular negative inner states. What setting or person, for example, brings up our competitiveness, fear, or shame? We may indeed be abandoned by others, but how does this manifest within us? How might we contribute to this outer experience?

I want to mention here the courageousness of this approach. We all carry within us the ability to be heroic, to access our fearlessness. Heroines don't rely on outer circumstances to define them or set things up for them. Heroines don't blame others or God. Heroines courageously take on their lives from the inside out, naming what interferes with a truly fulfilling life. Heroines don't give this power (superpower in my estimation) over to another. A priest, guru, counselor, teacher, parent, or even friend is not given permission to name our faults (or take our inventory, as they say in 12-step programs). Besides, no one knows you as well as you can come to know yourself.

This is a coherent exploration of a dynamic that keeps our true nature captive. This exploration is simply holding a conversation with some inner condition. We are willing to explore what causes our suffering, but we do it in a way that doesn't increase our anxiety and suffering but decreases it through compassionate awareness. The beauty is that when we explore in this way—compassionately, and with curiosity, not anxiety—we automatically discover what quenches the suffering. We discover that "an antidote is right next to the wound," as the popular African proverb goes.

Here are some simple steps to follow to choose and explore a dynamic on your own:

1. *Take some time to choose a dynamic, some inner state that interferes with your happiness and satisfaction, some habitual way that interferes with the forward movement of your life.* Typically, these dynamics are referred to as negative emotional states or reactive/habitual states. In actuality, these dynamics are a combination of emotions, beliefs, assumptions, and perceptions that we have come to identify with. In my book *The Wheel of Initiation*, I refer to our "pain stories." Pain stories are made up of agreements, assumptions, negative perceptions, and narratives that originated in our past. Here, we explore the narrative we hold around a certain dynamic.

Give yourself a week or so to identify the dynamic you want to explore. Consider which one, when transformed, would truly impact your life in positive ways. More examples of dynamics include: the need to take sides, attachment to results, chronic feelings of regret, the need to dramatize everything, distrust, having to live by "shoulds," living your parent's life rather than your own, an inability to forgive, white privilege, and arrogance.

A few years ago, I considered exploring the dynamic of doubt. What I quickly discovered is that I didn't have all that much of an issue with doubt. So I maintained a curiosity around the times that I found myself struggling. I asked myself: *What dynamic is either causing my suffering or contributing to it? What lingers here, causing me more pain?* I was both surprised and illuminated by what I discovered. The dynamic that kept coming up and that I consequently decided to explore was: how I hold others ransom with my expectations, or simply put, my expectations. Many strains of difficulty in my relationships had this dynamic at its core. I began with writing the story of this dynamic and found how pervasive it has been throughout my life. Thank goodness for compassionate inquiry because there were a few harsh realities attendant to this process.

I recommend that you, too, take time to explore in the same way I did. When struggling, take a look inside yourself and ask: *What is contributing to this difficulty . . . from within?* Once you discover a dynamic, explore more of its history and narrative through contemplation and witnessing.

- Jason, too, chose the dynamic of expectations. He chose this because "every time I expected someone to behave or respond a certain way, I became disappointed and resentful." I invited Jason to look at his expectations as a pointer to the full dynamic, rather than the dynamic itself. When he is disappointed in this way, what causes the most suffering? What lingers after the disappointment? What internal negative emotions, thoughts, and beliefs continue on after the occurrences are over? For him, resentment often followed his disappointments. He ended up choosing resentment as his dynamic.

Choose a dynamic that has a history for you and that you recognize as a place card for dissatisfaction, negativity, and suffering of some sort or another. Cultivation of such awareness alone will be liberating. In the above example, Jason felt freedom from his dynamic by simply going through the process of identifying it, as did I with mine! I feel serenity when I understand my suffering to be a result of my expectations and not what someone else did or didn't do. I can change my expectations; I can't change others to fit my expectations.

But don't stop here.

2. *After naming your dynamic, do some compassionate inquiry around its negative aspects.* How and where does this dynamic come up in your life now? How is it an obstacle to satisfaction, intimacy, creativity, happiness? How and where does it arise in your relationships? Where do you witness it in your surrounding social environments? Write out the story of this dynamic in your journal. Begin by asking yourself: what is the history of this dynamic in my family and childhood? Then explore how it came up in your teen years and beyond, up to the present moment. You may also choose to read up on a particular dynamic.[4] If you are not into journaling, simply contemplate the above questions.

3. *Next witness how the dynamic comes up in the daily context of your life.* Maintain a reference to this dynamic and how it arises in the moment. When I find myself facing difficulty and getting hooked by negativity, I bring my dynamic to mind and ask, "How is this dynamic interplaying with this situation?" Take some time to journal any related awareness or further questions to explore. Be willing to continue exploring this dynamic for a few months (or longer) or until you experience an internal and external shift around how the dynamic manifests. Again, the simple willingness to hold a curiosity around a particular dynamic will result in awareness that will bring about lasting transformation and freedom from negative states.

4. *At this point, explore ways to remain present to this dynamic without creating more of it in your life.* As you explore your

chosen dynamic, you will inadvertently discover antidotes because they are right there! What will organically occur is that you will find that an antidote is right next to the wound itself. Whereas we typically explore a dynamic for as long as it takes, in my year-long circles, we shift our attention and efforts to our antidotes about midway through the year. There is only so much "digging" we need or want to do to keep our lives in a forward motion; if we're not careful, we may spend too much of our time digging up dirt on ourselves when we need to be creating solutions and opening up to what is possible. I find that after practicing a particular mind-training technique, I don't have to keep digging for issues and unfinished stuff for long but can put my energy and attention on antidotes—the medicine that is next to the wound. As you uncover your dynamic and surrounding narratives, you are invited to also discover "antidotes and medicine" that make it possible to live more fully, more freely. At some point, you will put most, if not all of your energy on what you discovered is the "medicine" and will stop dwelling on where and how you have been wounded. You can become free of such states as shame and resentment because they are not natural, original states, that is, who you are at your core.

5. *Finally, after some time exploring your dynamic, name an antidote.* What is the medicine that lies close to the wound? For instance, in my exploration of expectations, I found that this dynamic created a quick way for me to falsely protect myself through disengagement. I had lost relationships due to my living this dynamic. The moment I became clear on how to let go of expectations and be receptive to the moment, every one of my relationships benefited. In fact, I found that new relationships emerged through this opening. I took the action of being receptive anytime I felt the tug of expectations arise.

When doing this inner work, you, too, will find that insights arise organically, given your willingness to maintain a curiosity to explore. When my dynamic of holding expectations tries to rear up (dynamics seem to have a bungee cord attached to them), its arrival automatically ignites my antidote of living receptive to the moment. But at first, when I discovered how active in my life was this dynamic of "holding people hostage with my expectations," my heart broke. I felt embarrassed and ashamed. Our explorations into a dynamic often will break our hearts. Fortunately, this internal work opens up an opportunity to effect a change in our heart. A consistent message in Parker's teachings is that we can choose to have our hearts either break apart or break open—open to the antidote.

You may want to explore, as we have above, a particular hindering dynamic as you move through this book. You will soon experience direct benefits of transforming negative dynamics into life-affirming antidotes. You will witness your heart breaking open.

As you explore and transform a chosen internal dynamic, become aware of actions you can take to help weaken the negative dynamic and strengthen the antidote. This, too, is an expression of living life from the inside out, living life from your side.

Our dynamics are part of our human experience. Being competitive, afraid, or jealous are qualities we can master, rather than have them master us. As Dr. Seuss says in *Oh, The Places You'll Go:* "We have brains in our head." We can use our brains to choose a way to soften the hold of such dynamics. We can reframe them: choose to be competitive with our past self; listen to our fears as a nudge to do things differently; understand our jealousy as a way of trying to protect ourself or loved ones. It's not so much about eliminating them, as it is illuminating them.

Just as our outer experiences reflect our inner life, as we walk the outer labyrinth of life, we also walk an inner one. I was taught in "therapy school" not to give clients guarantees. Well, I broke that rule long ago and do so here as well. (I have also discovered that there are free lunches and that there can't be too much of a good thing.) So I guarantee a personal and relevant realization simply as a product of your explorations.

THE INNER LABYRINTH

My father was a traveling salesman throughout most of my childhood. He sold packaging products to small local cheese factories throughout Wisconsin and the Midwest. This was a face-to-face affair. There were no scams or virtual exchanges in the mix. And he loved the sale. The "wealth" for him was in making the contact and in a successful sale. He did well, and at some point expanded into his own company and had others working for him. Even then he kept traveling to sell his products face-to-face. This made him a weekend father at best, which was typical back then for many working parents. My father had two axioms he swore by—and as far as I could tell, lived by: *everyone is selling something; and do your cold calls on Friday afternoons because most other salesmen have taken off early to golf.* For my father, the latter proved your work ethic and dedication to prospecting clients, while the former simply stated a truism.

You may understand the **Inner Labyrinth** as part of my sales pitch to you on the benefits of inner work. I hope to "sell you" on the advantages of living life from the inside out, keeping hold of your red thread. I want to successfully pitch to you the tangible rewards of bringing a continued curiosity to your life's journey and experiences. The benefits you will accrue will extend well beyond yourself into every encounter and community you are a part of. Guaranteed. An inclination to explore inwardly will lead you to your own personal experiences and conclusions. That is the whole point! You are not to have my experiences! Each of us will have a deeply personal and relevant spiritual awakening each time we explore a teaching or practice for ourselves.

The **Inner Labyrinth** gives us a simple visual of what happens as we explore the complex connections between our inner and outer lives. You can also use this visual as a tool to take you from exploration to personal realization around any chosen topic or dynamic. Results—fulfillment of some exploration—will at times feel spontaneous, but in actuality such benefits are due to your conscious choice to explore your inner and outer landscapes.

As you read on, I hope you will see that I too "show up on Friday afternoons" when others may have abandoned their efforts for a round of golf. (Golf, of course, is only a metaphor here; I had a very short stint of once enjoying the game myself!) I show up in that I share my walk with you, for I am still learning and benefiting in great measure from these teachings and practices myself.

> **The way toward that sacred mound—**
> **through clear skies and sunlit hills,**
> **at the exit turns sharp.**
>
> **Welcome! Welcome! They smile.**
> **Some want to help carry my bags.**
> **But the stone I carry is heavy**
> **and cold.**

START HERE—RETURN HERE

We start at—and return to—the point of exploration, which is the entrance to our **Inner Labyrinth** and, most importantly, inner truth. We bring a question or a dynamic to mind. As long as we are willing and able to explore a dynamic or question (any question!), we will move forward to realization, which means something affirmative has become true for us. If at any point we are stuck, resistant, confused, or have been distracted away from our subject of inquiry, we return to our explorer's mind by re-approaching the topic with curiosity.

This curiosity may be asking yourself: What is this loneliness about? What makes me truly happy? What is it I truly want? How does my dynamic come into play here? Where does this topic/concern/dynamic come up in my life? How can I be present for this experience without getting hooked by negativity? We can get quite specific with our explorations or, rather than make all sorts of assumptions or jump in "beliefs first," we can just be "spaciously curious." Positive movement happens on the spot when we frame our challenges and moments with a question. We give ourselves permission to simply explore a dynamic or an antidote.

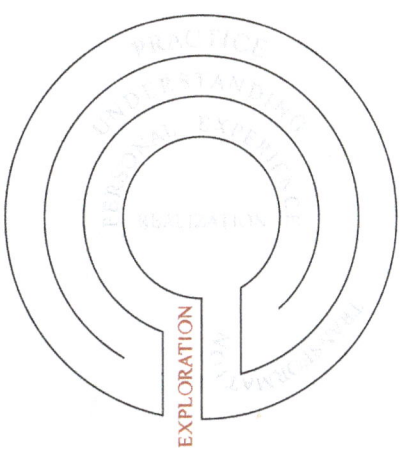

As I shared above, I chose to explore the dynamic of "holding others hostage with my expectations," which manifested as judgment and resentment in some cases. In my exploration of this dynamic, I discovered all the ways it came up in my life. Anytime I had a challenging moment or difficult encounter, I would ask: What's happening here? How might this dynamic be showing up in this situation? At this point we are not focused on positive results or outcomes—they will naturally occur, I guarantee. Instead, we are simply curious; we want to see how this dynamic, antidote, or question comes up in our lives. This means we are responding to situations with curiosity rather than with judgment.

DIRECT PERSONAL EXPERIENCE

Within the context of our daily lives, personal experiences happen that are a response to our exploration. These experiences are noticeable and tangible and bring with them a sense of connection to our spiritual source and to our life itself. Here we encounter and define our own experiences rather than letting others define them for us. As Parker said to me as we sat watching birds in his backyard: "Personal experience contains the guidance toward selfhood. All we need do is listen." Direct personal experience is the foothold of all of my and Parker's teachings. Our sanity, happiness, and integrity depend upon us listening to and trusting our direct and personal experiences.

- *When Henry explored a dynamic of codependency, he shared how he experienced "deeply felt encounters, which felt divine when I was also shown how I could do things differently. I know it was my efforts that made this change possible, but it felt divinely given."*

During my writing of this piece I had several synchronistic encounters with people who were being harmed by their involvement in some group or following. Each had one common dynamic that endangered their well-being: Their trust in their inner teacher had been severed, and they were not trusting their personal experience. One of these individuals was part of an outdoor shamanic training that presented itself as being "utterly unique." Leaders of the school constantly reiterated to their paying students that "this" was the "only place" one could receive this kind of teaching. The individual who called me felt he couldn't leave—though many others had, including a best friend of his—because he would "miss this one and only opportunity." This reminded me of the devastating story of the three people who died in a sweat lodge in 2009.[5] No one challenged the self-proclaimed guru or broke through the cloth walls of the sweat lodge. When the authority of another trumps our trust in our own personal experience, we are wholly in trouble.

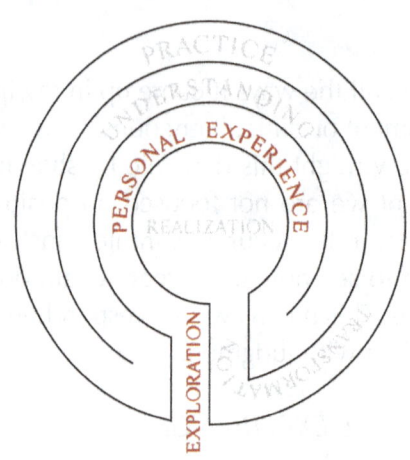

Over the years of my work as a therapist and educator, I have encountered too many people who have been diminished by a leader or someone else in authority. The shared dynamic in all these stories is the various ways the leader or teacher undermines their followers' trust in their own personal experiences. False leaders claim to have special knowledge or a special relationship with Spirit, so followers are to trust them in relaying Spirit's message to them. Thus they should not trust their own "inadequate" experience. This often makes the followers feel dependent on returning to this teacher for guidance and support. These false shamans use and abuse their students to fill their own pockets and egos.

One of my first teachers, Colleen Brenzy, said: "If you are feeling crazy, there is something crazy going on." She always emphasized, above all else, the importance of trusting your experience.

We all crave, to some degree, direct experience with spiritual truth. The more we explore from within, the more direct experiences we will have that wholly satisfy our cravings for such spiritual experience. Trusting our direct experience then leads to true understanding. I say true understanding because there is indeed a lot to be misunderstood or falsely understood. True understanding is solely based on our own personal experience rather than on someone else's interpretation of our experience.

Before we move on, I want to share another reason to trust your personal experiences even when they result in mistakes—as they sometimes will! When someone comes to me struggling to make a choice based on either their inner voice or the voice of others, I reassure them that mistakes will be made on either path they take. Mistakes are part of life. But the mistakes you make that are based on following someone else's choices for you will be very difficult to handle. Think of this as "their" path for you, thus the consequences are "their" consequences, "their" mistakes. You don't necessarily have the internal motivation or knowledge to handle "their" consequences. On the other hand, when you risk taking your chosen path based on your personal experience and motivation, everything that happens, including mistakes, will be manageable. Actually, the mistakes you make based on your own experiences and internal processes will likely be life-enhancing.

THE HEART OF UNDERSTANDING

Here our direct spiritual experiences, our meaningful experiences of feeling connected and "heard," develop into personal understanding. This is where we deepen our understanding of ourselves and the world around us. We perceive and comprehend things differently as a result of our exploration and personal experience. Our life situation improves based on this understanding. We gain the courage to act in ways that reflect this newly found appreciation of something. In such a state of understanding, we are able to make choices that express our integrity and our intentions.

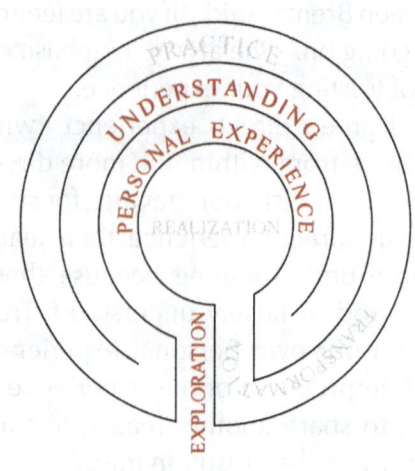

As I mentioned above, there are those I've worked with who felt utterly shattered by a spiritual teacher. Paradoxically, following and believing such a teacher is one's own mistake and one can come to own that mistake. Therefore, once owned, one can understand how to turn such fractures and sometimes years of misdirected spiritual and financial investment into a learning experience for oneself.

 **This house alive—creaking under cold pressures,
small fires within pushing back,
keeps timbers from cracking.**

PRACTICE: ACTIVATING AN ANTIDOTE

Here is where we integrate a chosen spiritual practice or principle. We choose to lead from an antidote, not lead from our more negative dynamics. We see the difference in this all the time when someone acts and leads from fear or competitiveness rather than courage and compassion. The intention here is to have certain spiritual principles and practices ready to use because once we hold an understanding from some dynamic, we will want to relate to this situation with integrity.

At this stage, we activate an antidote. What is an antidote to your dynamic? As mentioned above, most times an antidote arises organically from exploring a dynamic. We realize that an antidote to hate is some relatable expression of love; an antidote to jealousy is generosity; or an antidote to taking sides is realizing the promise of paradox and living in the **both-and**.

You may bring in one of the Five Habits of the Heart,[6] the practice of reframing (see Chapter 7), or any of your already chosen spiritual principles. I recommend the use of slogans (like those from the 12-step programs or Lojong teachings), antidotes, or certain spiritual principles memorized as a way to have them "in our back pocket" for easy retrieval. When we study and contemplate our spiritual and ethical principles, we find that they quite naturally show up on our path in response to our

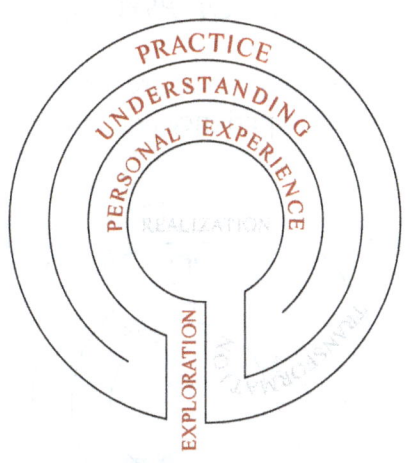

increased consciousness and understanding. In my book *The Wheel of Initiation: Practices for Releasing Your Inner Light*, the reader chooses their spiritual principles as part of their initiation. Having something to practice helps us to not get tangled up in outside circumstances. Instead, utilizing a given practice, we relate consciously and purposefully to whatever arises in our life.

Awhile after my blind dog died, I brought home a rescue puppy. My other, older Jack Russell didn't want to have anything to do with her. So I took my old dog to training to learn some new tricks. One of the tricks was to not let him go through a door ahead of me. And once he waited for me to pass the threshold, his reward was that he could come along. This is like our spiritual practices—let them lead the way, let them go ahead of you, and then follow them through the threshold. This creates an experience that is led by a spiritual practice.

Also, two of my all-time favorite practices for dealing with difficulty "on the spot" are choosing to become like a heyoka (page 52) and the Three R's of Touching Reality (page 65).

 **Light tapped the pane to wake me,
crossed the sill and out
splashing blue down a temporary path
and on.
What could I do but follow?**

SPIRITUAL OR PSYCHOLOGICAL TRANSFORMATION

Transformation is a direct result of our explorations, based on our personal experience and understanding, and from reliance on our personal practices. Transformation is not something we demand of ourselves or others. Overused in spiritual and psychological arenas, "transformation" is too often made as a promise after you put your money down. Too often others are out to "convert" you into their religion or view. The type of transformation we are talking about here, however, is a natural result of one's efforts. Transformation is experienced more as "becoming" oneself than as a "change" in oneself. Your dynamic of fear is transformed into courage. You become courageous.

In Japanese anime or *tokusatsu* dramas, *henshin* (transformation) is when a character transforms into a superheroine by speaking a catchphrase or using some transformative device or practice. Similarly, when we practice our spiritual principles we activate our own inner powers. Psychologically and spiritually, we experience transformation as both a transformation in how we relate to something and how we experience something. This kind of transformation is deeply rooted and abiding because it comes from within and is not in any way coerced from without.

REALIZATION

Realization will always result in some outer action that benefits us as well as others. Authentic realization will never just be about you or me individually. There is always interdependence at play. Even when we are deep into ourselves and working through something quite personal, realization includes an acknowledgment and experience of our connection to all that is and to each other. This is as courageous as it gets—where our explorations become medicine the world needs.

So with your arrival at the center of the **Inner Labyrinth**, the transformation that has taken root in you blossoms into more of who you are. And as you encounter the outer world, you have this realization now within you as part of your being.

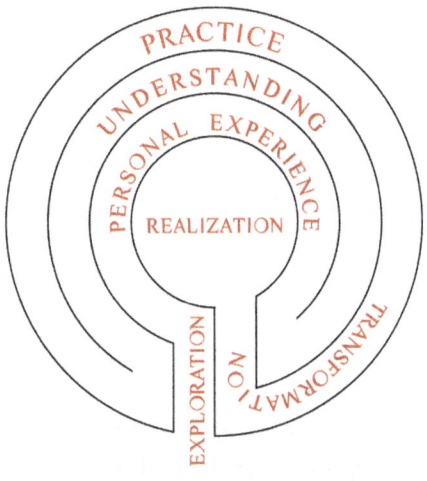

An expression in Buddhism is: "further becoming"—further becoming ourselves. This is not a one-time thing, one rebirth experience, but a continual birthing.

A BEAUTIFUL THING

I am blessed as I explore a dynamic, facilitate a Red Thread Circle while I write this book on the subject. So I admit this keeps me easily in conversation with a dynamic and other explorations! I want to share something that may help you to stay in the conversation, to remain present with your dynamic and explorations.

Transformation and realization come with keeping a dynamic continually and compassionately conscious, staying curious about how this dynamic is coming up in our life. We stay with the dynamic long enough to uproot it. Or, as I like to say, dismantle it. We want to understand the ways in which this negative dynamic trips us up, keeps us in an old story of ourselves and the world.

 **had I one thing I could change on this long,
labyrinthine walk,
I might more often think
to remove my shoes.**

Then, as we explore and are in conversation with our dynamic, antidotes naturally arise. We have to be conscious not to abandon our awareness around our dynamic when we discover an antidote. A continual and reliant practice of introspection can tame the mind and create a manageable and even beautiful life. We practice such active contemplation until we feel freed from a dynamic or it no longer drives our bus. The dynamic may be a backseat passenger, but it no longer drives our experiences. Negative states of mind may try to boss us around like a backseat driver, but they hold no real authority. We become fearless when we undermine our negativity and bring an antidote, such as compassion, into the world.

My dynamic for my first year's Red Thread Circle was related to grasping and attachment: strong attachment to what I want. While exploring my "strong attachment," I stumbled upon an antidote. Using the **Inner Labyrinth** as a guiding template, I arrived at an *understanding*. When I no longer had this dynamic driving my experience, I moved into the *practice* part of the labyrinth and brought an antidote intentionally out into the world with me; I arrived into *transformation* and *realization* where the dynamic no longer defined "who I am" and the medicine and antidote of "letting go" became my reality.

My antidote of "letting go" will be what I explore and express in the world now, as best I can, particularly when the dynamic of "strong attachment" nags me from the back of the bus.

And as we explore our inner life, we transform the world outside us from within, and that, Dear Reader, is a beautiful thing.

**Stop asking for the lamp to be put in your hand.
Pick it up, and fill it with your own oil.
It is the stuff of *you* that's meant to burn.**

CHAPTER TWO

UNWINDING THE THREAD: LIVING WITH CONTRADICTIONS

. . . to experience contradictions not as impediments to the spiritual life but an integral part of them. The contradictions of life are not accidental. Nor do they result from inept living. They are inherent in human nature and in the circumstances that surround our lives.

—Parker J. Palmer

Here we enter our metaphorical labyrinth and begin to unwind the ball of red thread (the teachings) with one foot in the labyrinth and one out. As such, we meet up with contradiction, for one foot is in the unknown world and one in the known. How true this can be in our lives!

We agree to take a risk and open ourselves up by moving forward and taking responsibility to live life from the inside out, only to find ourselves facing a contradiction. Our two worlds, as it were, will not always match up, nor will they ever easily match up. At this point, an inner dialogue with ourselves begins.

When we claim our contradictions and difficulties as part of our humanness and as integral parts of our spiritual journey, we turn difficulties into something workable. This is what I so love about living life from the inside out, and this is what ultimately empowers us: ***Everything that shows up in life is***

workable material. Nothing is exempt. We get to discover the promise of paradox for ourselves and have powerful and meaningful spiritual experiences based on our own stumblings and discoveries. Consider this Buddhist teaching: As long as you are stumbling, do your best to stumble forward.

With some contradictions, it may take a little inner work to recognize their paradoxical nature. Other contradictions rattle us to our core. When we experience contradictions, we need the support of a strong spiritual practice as well as the encouragement of others who may hold space for us as we discover our own inner knowings.

Bottom line—no matter what the breadth of the contradiction, its arrival can be a time to find the inherent paradox within it. Contradictions are rich with opportunity.

TRUE POWER VERSUS FALSE POWER

The turning of life's contradictions into workable paradoxes is essentially the process of honing in on our extraordinary, true powers. In one of my favorite books, *A Tale for the Time Being,* by Ruth Ozeki, the protagonist is shown how contradictions are an opportunity to use our true power.

> "Nattchan, I think it would be best for you to have some true power. I think it would be best for you to have a superpower."

She was talking in Japanese, but she used the English word "superpower," only when she said it, it sounded like "supahpawah." Really fast. "Supapawa." Or more like "SUPAPAWA—!"

> "Like a superhero?" I asked, using the English word too.
> "Yes," she said. Like a SUPAHIRO—! With a SUPAPAWA!" She squinted at me from behind her thick glasses. "Would you like that?"

Wouldn't we all like to own our SUPAPAWA? That's what this chapter and book is about—owning the inherent power to transform contradictions, to access what we are truly capable of, "to grow optimally according to the conditions of human existence and thus to become fully what one potentially is," as Erich Fromm wrote about in *The Art of Being*. Honing our supapawas of paradox makes our becoming possible. However, this way to relate to our circumstances and ourselves can completely upend us. Old held-onto beliefs, our habitual ways of being, as well as our dynamics are all challenged. A larger awareness of the paradoxes within our troubles leads us to see the messes of our lives with a much larger lens, and at even the best of times, this can make us feel unsettled.

> "Am I crazy?" she asked. "I feel like I am sometimes."
>
> "Maybe," he said, rubbing her forehead. "But don't worry about it. You need to be a little crazy. Crazy is the price you pay for having an imagination. It's your superpower. Tapping into the dream. It's a good thing, not a bad thing."
>
> "I mean, there are lots of superheroes with different superpowers, and some of them are big and flashy, like superstrength, and superspeed, and molecular restructuring, and force fields. But these abilities are really not so different from the superpower stuff that old Jiko could do, like moving superslow, or reading people's minds, or appearing in doorways, or making people feel okay about themselves just by being there."

We are much like the mythological superheroine when we engage our superpowers—not to walk through walls but to transform our difficulties into opportunities. Superman had to be a hero in secret; his public persona was that of a bumbling news reporter. Even the woman he loved could not see who he really was. That is why this journey is often referred to as the "hero(ine)'s journey." You wake up your true nature and true powers to bring your more awakened self into your community to benefit others; you don't do it for acknowledgment or recognition. Like Theseus, there's lots of paradox on the heroine's journey! Simply finding ways to be kind to the unfriendly stranger or patient when everyone around you is in a rush is a SUPAPAWA.

Results using these powers will be remarkable: "As we have the faith to live fully in the midst of these contradictions, we will experience resurrection and the transformation of our lives," Parker confirms. Sometimes, just knowing that the red thread of paradox is there is enough to get me through a difficulty. I do not recommend a vigilante hunt to find the paradox. Instead, live the question, ask, *What might be the paradox here?* What we need will be revealed. Exploring the question and being ready and willing to exercise our true power and innate wisdom takes covert courage, like that of our mythological superheroines. We appear as fumbling desk clerks by day but are true superbeings when needed.

A particular contradiction of "taking sides" holds at its center the motherlode of paradoxes. This principal paradox is the main vein of all paradoxes: instead of **either-or**, we can choose to live the contradictions, as we can find the **both-and** within our smaller and larger contradictions. Parker invites us to "refuse to flee from the tension" of such pivotal moments and instead "allow that tension to occupy the center of our lives."

This chapter offers favorite practices of mine as ways to face contradictions and to "live large" and intentionally through this promise of paradox. Such a promise is keeping hold of the red thread of transformation: "If we replace **either-or** with **both-and**, our lives will become larger and more filled with light" (PJP). For me, living by the paradox of **both-and** means challenging the ways we separate ourselves from our true (inner) selves, from others, and from the natural world. Now, at sixty, living in the **both-and** continues to reveal where I still want to be in control, where I rummage for the old habituated sense of safety in living divided and separated.

When I took on exploring this dynamic of **either-or**, I paid attention to moments when the most tension arose. I noticed where I stumbled and discovered that all my stumbling and suffering had one common dynamic: that of taking sides, of making things or people either right or wrong. Of course, I had also stumbled upon the quintessential paradox: living in the **both-and**. In the past, I have used the **either-or** dynamic as a way to protect myself, to live in the "fight or flight" mode of existence. Now, instead of relying on the **either-or** dynamic, I stay present within the tension of this contradiction. I found the **both-and**, the equanimous space of not having to do the **either-or**.

I quickly understood that this was an antidote, the highest place I could take these times of contradiction with the **either-or**. So I took this **either-or** dynamic into the **Inner Labyrinth** and explored its history and influence in my life. Not long after did I find myself at the center of this inner journey to a place of realization. During this same time, my daughter made her decision to attend a college whose theme happened to be The Power of And.[7] The synchronicity was not lost on me, and when this happened, I knew I had a dialogue going on with my true nature and with Spirit.

The promise of paradox is that we can take any of our dynamics of fear, shame, blame, jealousy, competition, feeling entitled—to name a few—and find their antidote in their paradoxical nature. This central paradox of **both-and** will be the red thread that helps you discover a specific antidote, the transformation of contradiction into paradox that frees you from being trapped by contradiction, trapped by having to take sides. This promise says for me that in reality there is no **either-or**; instead, there is always a paradoxical thread that runs through every contradiction, every dynamic. We just have to take hold of it.

Discovering **both-and** likely saved a friendship, made the "empty nest" full, and helped me to live life larger going into my sixties. When we are willing to explore what is truly possible, what is truly possible will be revealed to us. The trail of blessings makes living with the tension of such contradictions wholly worthwhile.

> **Of course you're not worthy.**
> **Of course you are, being**
> **from the mind of God.**
> **What is it you see—**
> **mud bound feet, frame bent and flopped,**
> **too soft ever to push open pink?**
> **Or a tulip?**

So when we explore the contradictions in our life, what do we see? Mud-bound feet or a tulip? We will get the personal insights and movement forward that could not have happened any other way. But herein is a warning from Parker J. Palmer not to misuse paradox: "Not all apparent contradictions are paradoxes in disguise, so discernment is required. The Orwellian slogan 'War is Peace' does not qualify, no matter how many presidents say otherwise." I would also say to those in an abusive marriage or a soul-robbing work environment: the paradox cannot be found by staying in the unhealthy, life-threatening environment but through leaving it.

USING YOUR SUPAPAWA: THE TRANSFORMATION OF CONTRADICTIONS INTO PARADOX

Whenever a contradiction presents itself, we have an opportunity: we can do what we always do, perhaps out of habit; or we can choose to open to and explore the contradiction. We meet a contradiction in the same way we explore a dynamic. A contradiction, however, often first appears in the outside landscape of our life: a disagreement with a loved one, an encounter with a tyrant, an online bully, an alcoholic spouse, to name a few. Living life from the inside out means we meet up with and respond to outside contradictions through our internal explorations. With a tyrant are you empowered or disempowered? Do you find yourself hindered by the internal dynamic of hopelessness? Are you stuck in taking sides? What do you do in an alcoholic relationship to care for yourself while not abandoning your loved one? Can you find the paradoxical thread when encountering a bully? Here we meet contradictions by exploring our inner landscape. We do this through the internal labyrinth of exploration (page 32) by exploring the contradiction (dynamic) that has presented itself and naturally discovering its antidotal paradox. In addition, we do this through the outer labyrinth (our outer lives) by acting on these awarenesses in our daily lives and relationships.

Instead of being in some habitual or negative state when someone is unkind or unjust, we can find the antidotal paradox that will transform the situation, at the very least for ourselves. We may not see the larger result—such as taking down a tyrant or restoring democracy—but we will add sanity and peace to a troubled situation. We act with fearlessness and compassion in response to contradictions. We focus our energy on the core paradoxical nature of reality. We live in the **both-and**. We refuse to sink to a bully's level.

I teach a master's-level social work class at the University of Wisconsin—Madison. My role includes placing students in their practicum. Now and then I find it hard to place a student. During a phone conversation with one particular student, she said, "I've talked with the other students, and they are not happy with you either." She made this point again before ending the conversation. That little drop of ink in water had now spoiled the coming year. I wasn't convinced that she spoke truth, but I was convinced, for a moment, that she could ruin the classroom experience for me. Then, I allowed for the paradoxical reality to emerge. And the **both-and** appeared along with the awareness that this student was presenting me a great opportunity to practice! She was a young woman starting her career as a social worker, whereas I was the elder, the mentor. I practiced not holding her to her comment. When we started class, I chose to meet her with fresh eyes and an open mind and heart. Later, at her first in-field evaluation, she took the time to apologize. What courage that took on her part! And I let her know that she gave me a wonderful opportunity to live my words. I remain grateful to her. She was a bright, kind, and attentive student. Had I gone into the class holding what she said against her, I am certain the outcome for her and me would have been different, not likely positive.

Each contradiction can present us with what I now call Leslie Moments. Be grateful for the opportunity! Search not for what's wrong; don't hold onto the them-me contradiction. Instead, acknowledge that this is an opportunity to learn and practice your spiritual principles, an opportunity to walk your talk and let your principles lead you through the door. If it weren't for the Leslies, how would we have an opportunity to practice turning contradiction into paradox? An **either-or** into a **both-and**? This is where the inner and the outer labyrinth meet: through our practice.

This living large can be challenging even with our smaller contradictions. In Buddhist practice, teachers recommend starting with small difficulties first. Practice with a smaller contradiction or smaller encounters in this dynamic, so when the larger difficulties and challenges show up, we have developed a means to be skillful. I was prepared for Leslie, prepared to meet her with an open heart instead of a shut mind because I had given years to my explorations and practice.

PRACTICE: A LESLIE MOMENT

Consider your dynamic—the one you identified in chapter 1—or a contradiction that is showing itself now, and explore how it trips you up in small ways. For me, a smaller version of "taking positions" is when I am attached to my opinion in the face of someone sharing their different perspective. I sense this internal tug of "I'm right; they're wrong." Or I feel an internal nudge that tells me to set them straight! Sometimes this appears in conversation when we are more focused on sharing our opinion than listening to the other.

A good friend of mine—and maybe you the reader—enjoys watching football. I find the game violent, an example of our society's misdirected passions (money) and mostly a waste of my time. I can easily slip into seeing myself on the high road here. So when a tug arises to judge others, I have an opportunity to present myself with an antidote of **both-and**. I consider the paradoxes inherent in this more benign situation. I see the enjoyment others get from gathering together and watching a game. I listen for what they enjoy and get out of watching football. Simply listening for what another appreciates is a great way to explore paradox in smaller, less challenging times.

It is good to have an idea, if not a full knowing, of what an antidote to your dynamic is. Thus, when you practice with small encounters of a dynamic and contradiction, you have an antidote handy. If you don't have a good idea of what an antidote is to your dynamic or contradiction, then a simple practice of wondering what it might be in these smaller, challenging encounters will be a great practice itself. This alone will reveal more positive ways to be in such situations. Simply ask: *What is a way to not get hooked by jealousy, anger, impatience?* Turn your adverse moments into Leslie Moments: *Where is the opportunity to practice, to strengthen my superpowers?*

- My friend Eric, columnist and community organizer, identified his dynamic as "always pleasing others." In his words: "My dynamic involves wanting to be liked, or more to the point, wanting to be seen as reasonable. This craving manifests itself in a draining mental exercise of rehearsing my winning arguments in my mind and practicing the punch line. When I explored this dynamic, I saw that this strategy doesn't work so well for me. Having practiced my punch line several times in my mind, I unleashed my impeccable logic on my sister. Her response: 'Eric, you're being a martyr.' She was right. Working with this dynamic seemed pointless; the more I thought about the consequences, the more I fell into the routine of practicing my reasonability. Then, during my morning meditation exercise, I noticed leaves swaying in the wind outside my window. Regardless of the strength of the wind, they always returned to their point of equilibrium, seemingly impervious to the forces around them. Herein lies a remedy. Conversation involves moving, a give and take with the forces around us. By listening to the other party, we take the focus off of ourselves, off the 'winning argument,' and onto a more fluid dynamic. It then becomes possible to be both consistent and flexible in our discussion, allowing us to return to our point of equilibrium."

So when we practice enough in the smaller versions of difficulty and conflict, our integrity muscle gets stronger and the paradoxical antidote more easily retrievable. We can even choose a bigger issue and watch how it arises in smaller versions. And!—even if I am right (let's say, for example, in the case of sending our young men and women to war, or the realities of climate change), I can still listen and relate to the other with an ear more finely tuned to the paradox that might be contained in their position. We can listen for something we can appreciate in them or in their view without needing to agree or disagree with them. That being said, this is not about being silent or not challenging bullies, negativity, or false views of reality. But when we challenge others from this more receptive place, I can assure you it has more power than if you were to "fight" from a place of revenge or taking sides. Take away the equation of winning or losing and instead focus on making contact, making a positive difference.

"TRAVELING TOWARD OUR DESTINY IN THE BELLY OF PARADOX"[8]

How do we keep ourselves open and receptive in often horrific contradictions? How do we open our hearts when depression or fear restricts us? How can this promise of paradox help us when a loved one is dying or we sense ourselves losing some grip on our understanding of what's meaningful? What might compassion look like in the face of human evil?

In T. H. White's *The Once and Future King*, Merlin says:

> You may grow old and trembling in your anatomies. You may lie awake at night listening to the disorder of your veins. You may miss your only love. You may see the world around you devastated by evil lunatics or know your honor trampled in the sewers of baser minds. There is only one thing for it, then: To learn. Learn why the world wags and what wags it. That is the only thing, which the mind can never exhaust, never alienate, and never be tortured by, never fear or distrust, and never dream of regretting. Learning is the thing for you.

As I work through the final rewrites of this book, we are eight months into the COVID-19 pandemic. This is a dark time with increased and overt violence, racism, gun shootings, and a president who divides and degrades. We are being broken. What we do in response to this brokenness individually and collectively will define our futures. We are at a very real and collective threshold. May our love for each other and our desire to heal and connect lead us through this threshold. This is a time (once again) to learn who we are, to identify and rely on our inner wisdom, and to choose where and how to be fearless.

This way, no matter what life gives us, we have a way to explore and open up to something other than the darkness and pain. We have to be able to find a way through and to act from our truths, no matter the outside circumstances. We can always learn, and from this learning know where and how to respond. When I am deep in a contradiction that rocks me to my core and may frighten me into extremes, I do what Merlin encouraged—I learn. Learning is the thing for me. And the way I have found to learn, to be a student in all that arrives and departs in my life, is to continue to explore. A learner is an explorer. In the previous chapter I presented the value of holding "an attitude of exploration."

We want to be careful not to become complacent and to just release the tension of our experiences. Our first need is not to release the tension but to live the contradictions, to be in this noisy, painful conversation with darkness, be it depression or a tyrant, or be it a dynamic that you have carried with you from birth.

THE PARADOX OF PRIVILEGE

Not until late in life did I come to understand how my life is framed by white privilege. In fact, this reality influences everything in my life. And if you are white—poor or not—this is also true for you. To reveal and benefit from the paradoxical nature of white privilege, we must explore what white privilege means within the context of our daily lives and how it affects our experience as a human being—a white woman in America, in my case. At some point, those of us who are privileged need to acknowledge this dynamic if we are to live an authentic life. White privilege isn't in and of itself a paradox; as with any dynamic, it holds within it a paradoxical narrative. And white privilege holds many paradoxical narratives. My privileged life doesn't mean I have always felt privileged. Therein lies a core paradox: we may have shame or fear, dynamics that drive our experience, but we may not be aware we have them. Once we realize that shame, for example, influences everything in our lives, we can begin to transform our lives. We can turn shame into self-compassion. This is true with white privilege too. Once we become aware of white privilege as a dynamic, we can live more honestly. We can be more fearless and compassionate. We can challenge this dynamic and own up to it through our beliefs, assumptions, and actions. Then, the second layer of paradox arrives: we still are privileged. With shame or fear, we may actually become wholly free of its influence on our lives. This is possible. At least such dynamics no longer drive our experience. White privilege has a culturally set context and cannot simply be shaken off with awareness or practice. The color of our skin—white privilege—follows us to our grave. Still, its paradoxical nature can help us live more honestly and compassionately. As long as we first maintain an awareness of how this dynamic is part of every experience, it may no longer secretly drive our experiences. As we challenge this dynamic internally, we can help change the outer landscape of racial injustices.

Herein arrives the third layer of paradox with white privilege: We can use our white privilege. We can choose to challenge racial injustices we encounter. We can speak up when we see someone being mistreated, bullied, or denied something because of their skin color.

This particular privileged state is just one.

In the words of this book's poet, Rebecca Cecchini:

> There are, of course, many privileged states in our world that could be paradoxically included in this thread, including male privilege, young privilege, hetero privilege, economic privilege (often stemming from the others). These and other privileges so often ride unimpeded under our awareness but affect others deeply. They are part of our social constructs and move through all of us, surfacing wounds as the many "isms" we don't personally wish to claim. Opportunity abounds here to make broader applications of the paradoxical lessons.

A worthwhile exploration for each of us may be to identify a particular privilege that is current in our life. There are simple approaches we can use to challenge and shift our privileged states and all of our contradictions to help us find contradictions' inherent paradoxes.

A REALLY GOOD TRICK: THE PARADOXICAL SUPERPOWER OF THE HEYOKA

Early on in my mind-transformation practices, I found myself at times inundated with certain dark thoughts that seemed to appear randomly and out of nowhere. They would show up at different times in my life and interfere with an otherwise pleasant time. They didn't seem to have any cause. Asking why they existed only generated more unhappiness on my part, so I decided to give more attention to when they arose. Knowing that an antidote is next to the wound, I noticed how, if it weren't for these random dark thoughts, I would be feeling connected to my experience at the time. In fact, they tended to show up at times that would otherwise be particularly pleasant.

At times of repetitive negative thoughts, we can choose to become like a *heyoka*, a trickster. I have shared this practice with countless clients and students, and they report back on the remarkable results. When contrary or other habitually negative thoughts arise in the mind, turn inward toward the thought and greet it. Then do a small bow and say to it: *thank you*. Acknowledge to yourself that *this particular thought or belief would not be arising if the opposite weren't actually true*. Then notice and open up to what is going on, touch the beauty of the moment. Turn your attention to your present experience.

You then become the trickster, a *heyoka* to the negative, habitual thoughts. You free yourself of a negative dynamic by not letting it block your view of reality, of the present experience. Instead, "the bowing to the contradiction" pulls you more deeply into reality because it becomes a flag that something beautiful, something real is actually happening right now.

Let's say you are enjoying a wonderful conversation with a friend, and you begin to have thoughts about what an idiot you are, or how bad you feel about your body, or you start having harsh thoughts about your friend, something along those lines. Identify these thoughts as flags and turn and face them. Bowing to them in gratitude, say inwardly, *Oh, thank you, you would not be showing up if something beautiful weren't happening. Oh, thank you, you would not be showing up if the opposite weren't true.* Then focus your energy and mind on, in this case, the reality of being with a friend. The *heyoka* has taken back the moment. Soon that particular flavor of negativity and contradiction haunting you from within will cease. You have tricked it into oblivion because the habitually negative thoughts no longer work to distract you from the moment. The negative mind stream can no longer undermine your true experience or connection with another. This trick actually invites the good in.

THE PARADOX OF INHERITANCE

One of the pivotal encounters with the promise of paradox came when I went to my Thai massage therapist because my knees hurt. At the time I was in my late forties. I considered this an inherited issue and was convinced that my troubled knees were inevitable.

We do inherit qualities and properties from our families and our ancestors. These can be physical or psychological pain stories. We inherit our parents' attitudes and genes, their worldviews and religion. My home was void of religion or spirituality, although my mother dressed us up on Easter Sunday for our annual trip to the local Lutheran church.

This was actually a blessing in disguise because this was where, at the age of eight, I encountered my first great spiritual teacher. One of my first lessons in paradox came from this particular minister, though I did not name it as such then. I was thirteen and had asked this Lutheran minister to baptize me. The minister instructed me to read and study the New Testament on my own and then asked me questions about it at our meetings. I admit that I wanted to be baptized because I had concerns about the afterlife and what would happen to me if I was not baptized. After several months of study and conversation, the minister and I got together one Saturday for my baptism. I was thirteen at the time. I sat in the room as he shared a few prayers and some doctrine with me. Then he got up to retrieve the holy water that I would be baptized with.

I sat in anticipation. I felt ready!

He reentered the room carrying a little bowl of water. When he saw the eager, expectant look on my face, he said to me, "It's only tap water, Julie." And then he said a few prayers and baptized me.

Only tap water.

Somehow, for me, this "only tap water" generated a more meaningful entrance into a new way of being than if it had been sanctified water.

The paradox that was seeded in me was profound. I began to wonder what it meant to be baptized with "only tap water." For me, this spiritual experience was profound in the way I related to it, not because some outside factor made it "holy." This brought both freedom and a deeper connection to "all that is." Much more became possible. I would call this my blessing of paradox.

This water that I'd been baptized with thus became both tap water and holy water.

Other inherited adversities in my life included alcohol abuse, a sense of entitlement, competitiveness, sensitive skin, narcissism, isolation, overeating, troubled knees, and arrogance, to name a few. Whenever any of us children got into trouble or experienced difficulties, the outside world was to blame. As I shared earlier, I inherited the belief that there are always sides to be taken; someone is either right or wrong. So what does it mean to inherit such characteristics that can ultimately define who we are, determine our destinies, and undermine our true strengths?

As a therapist for nearly four decades, I have come to appreciate that we don't have to claim the psychological qualities that were given to us. We can ask: *Who am I? What is truly mine? Who do I want and choose to be?* We may have inherited arrogance (insecurity disguised as arrogance) from our family, but we can choose how to be in the world. Everyone who comes in to see me has some issue that causes him or her suffering that has been passed down from his or her family. The greatest paradox in these inheritances is the gift they can bring us. Some of these gifts I received are described below:

- The lack of love and respect in my family motivated me to search for love and respect inside and outside of myself. My spiritual search began at the young age of eight and is how I came to be baptized at age thirteen.
- Although I inherited entitlement and "blamed others for any difficulties I encountered," I came to claim my superpower by taking 100 percent responsibility for my experiences.
- I created the eight-stage healing process, the Initiation Course, and the Zero Point Agreement from my contradictions and adversities.

Would I have explored and discovered my fearless and compassionate nature had it not been for my adversities? As I mentioned in the previous chapter, it is not so much about eliminating these dynamics as illuminating them.

Whatever our inheritances, we will be given the opportunity to claim an antidote that lies in the contradiction's promise of paradox. I have written quite a bit on how our troubles and troublemakers can be our best teachers. They present us with the contradiction of **either-or** and an opportunity to find the **both-and** paradox. Also, when we, or a loved one are confronted with such devastating news as cancer, Lyme disease, or debilitating arthritis, this is not about blaming ourselves or our histories. All we need at such times is radical acceptance of our humanity. We have both heroic powers and limits. We are **both-and** the heroine and the one needing help.

Now let's get back to my achy knees. Understandably, I still assumed, into my forties, that there were some qualities, like blue eyes, sensitive skin, and bad knees, that I had to learn to live with as part of my legacy. I went into my massage session wanting relief from the pain and left with a life lesson.

"I have bad knees that I inherited from my mother," I said to my therapist. My mother had had one knee replaced; the other was causing her problems.

"Don't agree to that," she said.

"What do you mean?" I laid myself down on the cotton mat on the floor. Thai massage involves pressure points, stretches, and massaging the clothed body. She placed her hand on my left knee, the one that was experiencing the most pain.

"The mind is a powerful anchor. Let your body be yours and not your mother's," she said.

I felt the release of **either-or** from my knees and in my mind. I let go of the thought that "my knees are like my mothers." I also chose some better shoes for my aging body, though I was fond of high-heeled boots. At this writing, twenty-some years later, my knees are strong and show no sign of problems—aging, yes.

Our curious and receptive mind, in a world full of contradictions, can be a mighty anchor.

> **As she walked
> on** land, tilted skyward,
> head firmly in clouds,
> feet afloat on firm ground,
> **so could she hear**
> in the in-between, all at once and distinct,
> **the jet plane and the cricket.**

CHAPTER THREE

BAREFOOT IN THE LABYRINTH: PENETRATING ILLUSION THROUGH ACTIVE CONTEMPLATION

Contemplation is any way one has of penetrating illusion and touching reality.

—Howard Thurman

That definition opened my eyes to myriad ways I might lead a contemplative life—as long as I keep trying to turn experience into insight.

—Parker J. Palmer

Contemplation doesn't always occur in a peaceful state of mind.

—Rebecca Cecchini

TURNING EXPERIENCE INTO INSIGHT

This is the first turn, the first edge in our metaphorical labyrinth. If we were to let go of the red thread, we might get lost in the outer appearances of twists and turns that arise in our life, perhaps even going over and over the same worn path—or problem—only to arrive at the same turn while never truly moving forward. We might see such edges as stopping points, a dead end of some kind, rather than a corner to turn. We would likely not gain much awareness from our experiences if we met such twists and turns without the thread of insight. But if we could understand these edges and turns in life as places of discovery, as times to slow down and consider our choices, we might notice our chance to turn this experience into something workable.

The premise that studying is an aspect of practice is contained in both Parker's teachings on active contemplation and in Buddhist teachings on Lojong practice (mind training). To explore is to study. To study is to contemplate. Study can challenge our "deceptions of self and world," says Parker. Active contemplation as a form of study means to explore ideas and principles for ourselves, figure things out for ourselves. Study can also mean investigating how our dynamics arise at our edges, surveying our ethical and spiritual principles, and reading these red thread teachings. Sometimes the study of one subject leads to an unexpected insight.

When we arrive at some edge where choices are required, we need to actively contemplate so we can make choices that are life-giving. At such edges in our life, we can't typically take a break from our daily routine. We need to find ways to penetrate illusion and touch reality within the context of our daily life, at our edges and corners. But in order to contemplate, we have to slow down enough to reflect. This far into our personal work we've come to rely on living life from the inside out in a life that is full of contradiction.

HOSTING THE EDGE

When we find ourselves at an edge, life has brought us to a turning point. We can choose to have our edges be places where we get stuck, avoiding whatever is going on in our lives, or ideally, our edges can be places where we slow down and take notice. At our edges there may be resistance, contradiction, expectation, and likely a mix of hope and fear.

We want to become better and better hosts of edges and turns. Using the imagery of being barefoot for a moment, we want to feel the ground beneath our feet as we stand at the edge of our contradictions, tense emotions, and life experiences. There we can sense the sharpness of the edge along with the curve of **both-and** at the point where we can turn a corner. To make the turn, we have to be able to slow down, take notice, and contemplate in the moment, so we can give our full attention to what's going on. *Active contemplation is the means by which we host our edges, leading them to become navigational points of reference rather than points of resistance.* So many programs and spiritual teachers promise enlightenment and freedom, but our very own lives offer this up to us for no extra charge! Not only this, but our ability to host our edges through active contemplation—by relating to our contradictory edges in this way—makes forward movement possible.

Our edges come up in the shape of our dynamics and the contradictions they may contain. They are flavored with our difficult emotions of anger, jealousy, righteousness, and fear. Our edges are our expectations, disappointments, mistakes. Our edges are felt in our relationships with others. They trigger our pain stories—deep-rooted untrue narratives we carry about ourselves and the world. Our edges often trigger habitual, reactive states. They often show up when some choice asks to be made. Our edges hold the tension between illusion and reality.

> **Bare foot sets down
> on soft ground.
> Familiar ring the bells that called
> you and you
> to come wander again
> through the rough
> internal terrains,
> looking always for the Word.**

Hosting an edge is about "being with the edge" without getting stuck or falling into some habitual way of relating to situations that the edge presents. Edges hold opportunities to challenge old, patterned ways of ours that are related to difficulties we've experienced in the past. In something like a divorce or a conflict within your community, the edge is likely wide and long-lasting. Some edges are less stretched out, but both quick ones and extended ones can be sharp, as in an argument with someone at work. Over time, through dedication and contemplation, the edges become less sharp and wide. I actually rely on these turns and edges to remind me it is time to slow down and actively contemplate the situation. It's time to study.

We want our actions to be based on discernment—discernment made through contemplation and reflection—because this ultimately leads to that happiness we seek. In our conversation around this, Parker said, "The quality of our contemplation dictates, to a considerable extent, whether we find life pinched, cramped, and fearful, or open, expansive, and free."

Most edges have some historical pain story at their core. A pain story is an outdated, often wholly inaccurate narrative we carry about ourselves. This story of our self or the world can hold a lot of influence. Our collective pain story of "having to choose sides," discussed in a previous chapter, can arise at every one of our edges. These pain story narratives are not true to who we are and what we are capable of, and they are often not true about the world and the people around us.

I was born into catastrophe, bound to two chronically angry and unhappy parents who took solace in alcohol and partying. I was caught up in an environment of entitlement, privilege, consumerism, and drug abuse. My father abandoned us through work and allegiance to another family. My mother spoke in contradiction by blaming others for her unhappiness, but when difficulty was brought up, she responded with: "Accentuate the positive; eliminate the negative."

I had to find a way to live among such contradictions without being utterly broken. In Buddhist philosophy there is a claim that it is these very difficulties and contradictions that can bring forth our best nature. I find this to be true. At my earlier edges, I had to choose either the world my family presented to me or the world I believed to be available to me. At the age of sixteen, I gave myself the opportunity to choose between the path my brothers and parents showed me and the opportunity to forge a path for myself. I was introduced to marijuana at the age of twelve by a cousin, but I gave up marijuana, began my meditation and journaling practice, and discovered the *I Ching*—an ancient Chinese oracle—all in the year I turned sixteen.

I have consulted the *I Ching* regularly over the last four decades, and I continue to do so today. With its guidance I am always given a way to study my predicaments as well as find a way to approach them in a principled and mindful way.

During my tumultuous early years, I learned to survive by making things black and white, right or wrong. I would not have survived that environment had I not made distinctions wherein my family's choices were "wrong" and mine were "right." The difficulty came when I stepped out of the family environment and took this survival tool with me. Now this edge of **either-or** is consistently a turning point, a place where I consciously attempt to replace the **either-or** with some version of **both-and**.

Active contemplation means to slow down enough to become present when things get edgy and difficult. We study some spiritual principle (I consult the *I Ching*), write in our journals, read and contemplate a poem or teaching story, or simply slow down and pay attention. Breathe.

Active contemplation helps us to "penetrate reality," even at the most difficult of times. Active contemplation is not something we force as a dogmatic practice but something we recognize as an inherent capability.

Over the years I have gleaned various ways to host the many edges that arise in my life. I offer my two favorites in this chapter. The contemplative practice is one that helps us not only free ourselves from our past—or from reliving our past—it also helps us gain insight through experience.

> **In the raw open place
> where hope rises
> to dissolve again the many
> times over,
> the sharp sting of *have faith!*
> smarts as it hits edges,
> aches as it goes deeper
> reminding
> how healing first hurts.**

CONTEMPLATIVE PRACTICE 1: HOSTING THE EDGE THROUGH AWARENESS

Our edges can be sharp with emotions and reactive states. We all have narratives and beliefs as well as traumas that get triggered when we find ourselves at the corner of a contradiction. To host an edge is to be present for the experience and to approach it with awareness. With this simple practice, we can turn our emotional edges, trauma triggers, and contradictory experiences into turning points that may have profound and lasting results—again, realization and freedom made from your own life.

In Zen practice a series of ox-herding images illustrate how our mental and emotional states relate to our well-being. The first picture is of a monk being dragged across the ground because he won't let go of the rope that is attached to the ox. We have all been like that monk, either not willing or feeling unable to let go of our habitual states. The monk is bruised and beaten, but he still hangs onto the rope. In the next image, the same monk has the ox tied to a large tree. They are both "stuck," as it were, in that one place, but the monk has successfully identified the problem. In the third image of the same monk and ox, the monk is happily riding on top of the ox. Here he has become master of his emotional and mental states. None of us want to go through life bloodied and bruised when we can be like the monk who rides triumphantly atop the ox.

Try This: How to Host the Edge

First, let me invite you to approach "hosting the edge" as an experiment. This gives you permission to simply learn, to see what happens for yourself. I can tell you that this practice has worked for me as well as for countless clients, but the proof will be in your own personal experience. And here is a caveat: Just this willingness to experiment will bring some relief. Trying this will be like giving yourself a bigger view out a larger window.

When you are feeling an edge of difficult emotions, start this experiment by bringing awareness to the emotional/habitual state. Imagine stepping back and just letting the emotion be without adding any storyline to it. Be a witness to this emotion. Ignore the routine thoughts that arise. Instead, host the edge and witness all the different sensations that arise in the emotional and physical continuum. This practice is much like watching the breath and other sensations in a mindfulness practice. You host the inner experience and don't lose yourself in the story or intense sensations that are arising in the body. Do your best not to name, label, or build any kind of story around the experience. Let yourself experience the various states surrounding it without responding to the inner experience in any way. Most internal edges are triggered by some outside circumstance, some of which are known, some not. Here, be willing to just be with the inner experience and its attendant sensations, whatever they are.

Whatever sensations are felt, stop talking to yourself about them. Realize that they are "just emotions," just sensations"— "just" in that they are not proof of anything. Our emotions are not in themselves a call to action; these are simply emotions, energy in the body, or physical sensations. Let yourself be with these emotions "just" as they are, even though your ego— and habitual self—will tell you to do something, now!

Don't act on these emotions and sensations while the intensity is present. You will find that the intensity and negativity are, like everything else, ephemeral. And emotions shorten and decrease every time we approach the same edge in this way. Along with the decrease in the intensity of emotions, the narrative winds down too. They are in many ways attached to each other; the narrative keeps the emotion going, while holding onto the emotion keeps the story going. As you are thus passive and not invested while hosting the edge in this way, the edge begins to round out; you turn this sharp edge into a passable corner. This is a way not to repress or suppress emotion. And this allows you to feel intense emotions such as regret or grief while not letting them develop into chronic sadness or regret. Also, you can then respond to circumstances without being reactive.

Next bring your attention to the edge, which has now been transformed into a turning point. Your mind and heart are open now to this present point where an antidote presents itself or you naturally just move on to something else—you turn the corner. What often happens is that you reach the end of the negative state and find yourself in something else. After the emotion is released through presence, and even though you know it will return or that it hasn't been entirely released, you can choose to draw your attention to an intention or spiritual principle, or return your awareness to the present experience. What principle or practice would help you take the next step? Or, if you are at work, having lunch with a friend, or simply hanging out at home, return your awareness to the present experience. But every time the emotions of fear, hostility, anxiety or even panic, regret, or loss arise, you can host the edge in this way.

CONTEMPLATIVE PRACTICE 2: TOUCHING REALITY THROUGH ACTIVE CONTEMPLATION

Nature continually points to how to be fearless and compassionate. Nature doesn't ruminate or move backward. And there is a common denominator throughout all life on this planet that reassures our place among the bravest, the healthiest, and the happiest. All life on this planet is entirely dependent upon receiving. Before we can give, before we can experience or provide love, service, kindness, or abundance, we first must receive such things and receive abundantly. If we do not learn to receive and to become receptive, we will either wither away or act in ways that are not truly life-giving. Health, light, insight, relationships are all things we have to receive in order to give. We can be in this beautiful, abundant world and still starve spiritually and creatively. We can be with others and feel utterly alone. When we don't know how to receive, we are like a hungry ghost, having small mouths where all nourishment just passes through us. We are then in a chronic state of hunger, what Parker refers to as the Empty Self Syndrome (pages 75–80). We may even become president of the United States but feel unfulfilled because we are not truly receiving what is given to us; we see what we don't have, thus crave for more—more money, more recognition, more control. This makes us a danger to self and others.

So we want to be receptive to the abundance, want to be able to receive reality. We want to recognize what is truly possible in our lives and be receptive to these possibilities. We want to receive insight, love, wisdom, and all the resources and beauty of this world. Often people come to me saying they are feeling stuck, tired, or unsure of themselves. For each of them, and for myself as well when I am going through a difficult time, it gets down to where we are resistant, where we have closed off our ability to receive. Much of our dissatisfaction, unhappiness, troubles, and conflicts come down to not being receptive to what the moment is offering us.

In the natural world, receiving and giving is an innate state, like breathing in and breathing out. The first breath we take is one of breathing in—taking in breath, receiving life. When we receive correctly, we also give what is ours to give instead of offering things that are not ours to give. We are not born into this world with an unlimited supply of gifts and possibilities. We are bound to the natural scheme of things too! This is great news. We don't have to go in search of who we are and what our purpose is. We just have to learn how to receive what is here already and what is offered to us. We don't have to struggle to figure this all out. We just have to learn to be receptive to ourselves, to others, and to the natural order of life. When we are in a state of receptivity, a state of receiving, we can touch reality and understand what we can give, what we can do in any given situation. I suppose some would call this "being present," but it is more active than that. Touching reality takes a disciplined mind, one that is willing to open and recognize the truth in the moment.

The Three R's of Touching Reality

1. ***Recognition.*** Recognizing the reality of the moment. What is this situation really about?

2. ***Receptivity.*** Opening and being receptive to the reality of the present moment through the practice of principles. Not letting some habit or negative internal dynamic determine our actions and the experience.

3. ***Receiving Reality.*** Receiving (touching) reality. And in our receiving we are able to give.

I came up with this practice through my encounter with His Holiness the Dalai Lama. A dynamic that often played out in my life and prevented me from receiving life's abundance was that of feeling competitive, thus often left out; I learned there was only so much love and attention to go around. In 1995 I was at a reception for His Holiness in Madison, Wisconsin, and I was fortunate to be at a small gathering of around 200 to receive him. We waited for him in the local Unitarian temple where a catering service had provided sweets and tea. The energy was intense. Most of the food untouched. Everyone was in anticipation of his arrival, and when he arrived, I found myself on the side of the path made for him. Behind me a man was shouting, "Your Holiness, Your Holiness!" and in his hand he held a bouquet of flowers that jetted out past my face. He sounded like he was in pain.

Then I asked myself: *What is this about? Is this about me being seen by His Holiness or is this about compassion and kindness, the core teachings of His Holiness the Dalai Lama?* The answer was sweet and simple: it was about practicing kindness; it was about generosity. So I stepped back, and the man happily took my place on the side of the path in front of me. When His Holiness came by, he reached around the large man, smiled at me, and squeezed my shoulder. All this simply from asking and opening to what this is truly about. His Holiness gave a short talk on the Tibetan cause and being kind to one another. Then when he was to leave, another path opened up, and I found myself on the side again. And again, a woman behind me cried out "Your Holiness, Your Holiness." It was a natural response at this point to let her have my spot. And again, as His Holiness went by, he reached around the woman, squeezed my shoulder and smiled at me.

I have used this practice in other situations where I felt the snag of negative desires or was confronted with difficulty or negativity from others. I have offered this practice to those in a variety of socio-economic backgrounds and a diversity of settings, all of which have found this not only useful but transformative.

First we ask: *What is this about?* Then we can naturally move into being receptive to the reality—an answer to that question—

> **From root's reach to heaven's foothold,**
> **all along spindled limbs**
> **rose a gentle peace,**
> **shook free**
> **from the tips of leaves,**
> **and poured down in,**
> **through the looker's eyes.**

and touch reality. Something certain and real takes place. To touch reality we reach a place, even if briefly, where we are in sync and in touch with all that is.

All we have to do to gain the power to recognize reality is to ask ourselves and explore the question: What is this about? Not *What is happening here? What do I want? What should I feel? What should be happening?* or *Why do I feel disappointed?* Ask *What is this about?*

Is this about winning the race, or is it about me enjoying the run and doing my best? Is this about getting her to like me, or is this about recognizing my true feelings? Is this about being recognized or about community? Is this about competition or cooperation? Is this about blaming others or about finding a way to be true to self and situation? Is this about proving a point or is this about . . .

Next we open ourselves to receive reality and whatever comes with it. Much like hosting the edge, we host the moment, becoming receptive to what the experience is truly about. This is beyond just cognitive and becomes physical, energetic, and relational. You could understand this as the practice part in the **Inner Labyrinth**. Here our spiritual principles help make us more receptive to what is truly being offered to us. This is where we don't let the past determine our present experiences and choices. This is where I stepped back after realizing that "what this is about" is generosity and kindness. I stepped back, becoming receptive to reality, and then received the gift of that practice and moment. And you will too.

Then we receive. We touch reality, and in our receiving we experience the reciprocity of life! Like breathing in and breathing out are dependent on each other, when we receive, giving naturally occurs.

LOSING ANOTHER ILLUSION AND TURNING THE CORNER

The benefits of hosting our edges and losing our illusions go way beyond our ability to navigate our own edges; the rewards can extend to such a point that we become skillful at being present with others' edges. We learn to be a witness rather than a referee when others are at their edges because we know and trust the effectiveness of simply being present and not interfering with another person's inner work.

If life is constantly made up of sharp edges, something big needs to change. No amount of internal work on our part will transform bullies or angry spouses into companions worthy of our life energy. No amount of meditation will replace voting in an election. This would be like me expecting the invasive species of garlic mustard to magically disappear if I simply imagine it gone. I am going to have to get down on the ground and pull it up by its roots if I want to improve the status of our woodland.

Nevertheless, *our duty is to our own integrity, an integrity that is fed from within. As we drop another illusion and turn this corner, we explore and define ways to feed our true nature through the inner aquifers of solitude, creativity, and purpose.*

> **Gathering senses,
> a wordless gauze to soften and hold
> the raised edge. Just wait here—at least
> till the swelling stops
> or while you figure it out,
> how to figure it in.**

CHAPTER FOUR

THE LABYRINTH'S AQUIFERS: THE WELL-FED SPIRIT

You know how robins run about eight inches, then stop, cock their heads, and look and listen? If nourishment is there, they find it. My soul offers continual guidance and sustenance, if only I will stop and listen, often.

—Parker J. Palmer

Here is where we pause to consider nourishment for ourselves and others. What we put into our bodies is obviously important. More significant is what we feed our mind and spirit and what the source is of this nourishment. So we pause and notice what we take refuge in, and how and with what we nourish ourselves. We pause and listen from our bodies—like the robin.

Just as we need to slow down to skillfully host our edges, we don't want to rush through the labyrinth of our life like a hungry puppy who heard the food bag being opened. That hungry puppy doesn't slow down enough to grasp what she is truly hungry for and often becomes what I later identify in this chapter as a hungry ghost—one who is always empty and always hungry because what it feeds on is not life-giving. The only way to be well fed is to be able to know what we are truly hungry for, to sense and discover that nourishment right under our feet.

Now that we have turned a corner, now that we know how to host our edges and touch reality, let's continue to walk forward, paying attention to what we truly want. *The richness of our life comes from making meaning with what arises day to day, moving forward with increased clarity of who we are and what truly nurtures us.* But this can't be done in a chronically rushed and stressed manner; nourishment can't be outwardly drawn when we worry about what others think of us or whether others approve of us. Discernment of what will nourish our true self depends, in part, on time spent in solitude.

**Night's spacious, still air
lets tightbound words uncurl from sidelines, to spread
outward freely over open trails, once crowded
in day's stampede.**

FACING INTO OUR HUNGER THROUGH SOLITUDE

An aquifer is an underground layer of water-bearing permeable rock or rock fractures from which groundwater can be extracted using a well. The key requirements for successful water extraction are having an aquifer that is at least partly below the water table and that has sufficient storage capacity and permeability to transmit the water.

Nature again reveals to us what we need to know to tap into those inner places of replenishment and nourishment. We, too, must have sufficient storage capacity and permeability to live from the inside out. Just as aquifers must be fed by rain and snow, our true nature must be replenished and nourished from without, from whatever we consider our spiritual source: the natural world, relationships, and meaningful vocation. We must receive all the blessings and nourishment that living from the inside out does for us. Our inner aquifer can only be replenished through times of solitude and silence.

An aquifer fills with rainwater or water from melted snow that drains into the ground. In some areas, the water passes through the soil on top of the aquifer; in others, it enters through joints and cracks in the rocks. We too must let the rain and snow of what nourishes us drain into us, whether through our strengths or cracks, through our assets or mistakes. Our true self is the solid rock in which the groundwater is held (paradoxically) within our fractures, joints, and cracks. The water stored in our aquifers may be brought up and out to the surface where it is shared via access to wells—wells that nourish our life and all life around us.

The traditional phrases "to give is to receive" and "it is better to give than to receive" are misleading. Notice how in our culture we have been taught to say "giving and receiving" as if giving is primary and receiving is secondary. But to give we must be wholly able to receive first, as described in the previous chapter. Nature consistently points to how it is in our receiving that we can give. Just as an aquifer is fed from the rain and then feeds the well, sun and water feed a plant, which then bears fruit that, in turn, provides nourishment.

Thus to be able to nourish ourselves and others, we must be like the aquifers that rely on a source that feeds it. This way we are capable of giving to ourselves and others honestly and fully because we are always connected to and benefiting from our source, both inwardly and outwardly. This also points to what we feed ourselves. Are we living on true sources of nourishment or falsely packaged "foods" that lack nutritional sustenance? This is what makes the journey inward—living life from the inside out—and the contemplative life so valuable; they help us to be in a reliable state of receiving and giving. Aquifers can dry up when people drain them faster than nature can refill them. Parker reminded me as I confronted time alone during the pandemic that, approached in a kind way, "solitude allows us to receive ourselves as we are." He shared that it is in solitude that we can receive because we are not continually distracted and consumed by what others expect or want from us.

Much like the saying that a bird can't always be in flight, we cannot always be busy searching for our purpose and identity. We can't always be planning and doing. Our body, mind, and spirit rely on solitude and aloneness for restoration and health. Without solitude, we cannot listen to ourselves, and without listening, we will not know how to listen, like the robin, for that sweet worm beneath our feet. Even what we most want will elude us because, as research shows, chronic busyness doesn't increase our satisfaction but decreases it. Those who are afraid of solitude, of being alone, of pausing and becoming aware tend to rush through their lives and miss the many treasures that only solitude can bring. As John O'Donohue shares in his book *Anam Cara*: "Only in solitude can you discover a sense of your own beauty."

Creating solitude is about cultivating an inner quiet. Finding solitude can be challenging in this world of "can you hear me now?"—smartphones, wireless access, Twitter, Facebook, texting, and Snapchat. But a busy life is also full of needed tasks such as taking care of family and pets, work, laundry, and community.

Solitude can be a time for active contemplation or simply a time of rest. This time with ourselves is typically accompanied by some insight. Meditation and purposeful resting, as found within times of solitude, give the body, mind, and spirit a much deeper quality of restoration than a nap.

LETTING THE GOOD SEEP IN

When my daughter was younger, we would finish some activity and she would inevitably say, "What are we going to do next!?" Maybe she got this from me! She liked—and still likes—to plan ahead. At these in-between times I would encourage her to take time to stretch out the latest good time through rest and quiet alone time. Let the good settle in, as it were. Just so, Dear Reader, when you have recently transformed a sharp edge into a corner and you are, for a bit anyway, at an easier passage, this is a good time to stretch and let the good settle in.

A wonderful practice of contemplation is to ask yourself what brought you to this time in your life—reflect on what got you to this moment.

For my daughter and her generation (she is now twenty-three), removing oneself from the Internet is and may be the easiest path to solitude but may also be the hardest to obtain. There were times when I called her on the phone when she was at college, and I would ask her, "Hey, what you up to?" And when she would respond, "Nothing," it typically meant she was online. I fear for the generation that hasn't had to wait for regular old snail mail to hear from friends and family and doesn't have to stand in line to wait for anything; texting gives us immediate access to anyone, and most things can be ordered online. These gaps and states of waiting without doing are restorative and informative. We need our "doing nothing" time to mean just that.

Natural gaps in our lives that can provide some solitude include waiting in line, taking a break between tasks, finishing up a meal or some other activity—those moments when nothing has been planned, those randomly occurring times of boredom. We can use times of boredom that arise organically in our lives as a time to "stay still" with the quietness instead of attempting to fill it up. Boredom tends to scare us, thus what too many of us do is fill up our time instead of using time to rest and reflect, to just be with ourselves or others in solitude. I attribute some of our nation's obesity to this; we don't know how to be bored or hungry without rushing to fill ourselves up with food, texting, or some version of activity.

We must find ways to notice the worms beneath the surface of things, to feel from our bodies what will truly feed our hunger.

> *When was the last time you were bored—truly bored—and didn't instantly spring to fill your psychic emptiness by checking Facebook or Twitter or Instagram? The last time you stood in line at the store or the boarding gate or the theatre and didn't reach for your Smartphone seeking deliverance from the dreary prospect of forced idleness?*
>
> —Maria Popova, "How We Learn to Be Alone," *brainpickings.org*

There is room, yes.

Stop living in your smallest self.
That's not who you are, always tight, pushing against
the limits of your poor little shell.
It takes no effort to see, really see, from here.
And you—salt and spark,
you step easily into greater heights
when you remember
there is room

TRY THIS: FIFTEEN GOLDEN MINUTES

We can start small. In fact it is best to start small. Many clients complain about not having time to be creative, to write, to play their instrument, let alone be quiet and listen to themselves. Yet they are aware of this need to tend to self, to engage in things that truly feed them, that replenish their inner aquifer. Here is what I do and what I recommend to anyone who has lost this in their life: Identify fifteen golden minutes where you will rest and listen, where you will work on your novel or attend to that one creative, nurturing act that is for you. Fifteen golden minutes to journal. Fifteen golden minutes to be outside in the elements. Fifteen golden minutes to play on your instrument. Don't commit to any more time than this—but do commit to this. Identify the time during the day when you will give yourself these fifteen golden minutes, whether it be something you commit to every morning or is part of your monthly calendar. You can, if you wish, choose a time that could segue into thirty minutes or more. When you pick your fifteen golden minutes, consider choosing a time that could become even more golden time for your nourishment.

TRY THIS: BREATHE AND NO EFFORT

"I get so angry every time you say that to us!" a client said to me during a session. She was also in my Red Thread Circle at the time where I offered this basic suggestion: breathe and no effort. She was actually working on not feeling so responsible to everyone and everything. She was overwhelmed and tired.

"What do you mean," I asked.

"Breathe *into* No Effort really pisses me off."

"It's Breathe and No Effort," I said.

We both got a good laugh from that! For the whole intention of Breathe and No Effort is to let go of pushing and shoving our way through our life and instead let go, breathe, let your natural way of being emerge. This allows for a gap in our doing and thinking, for small gaps of solitude through breath and effortlessness. Like the robin, just breathing and noticing. This state of "just being" gives us a way to accomplish all we want. Every lesson we want to learn, every idea we are studying, every spiritual practice and encounter can be approached with just Breathe and No Effort (no force), just presence and engagement. Open up to the natural nourishment of breath. Breathe, let go ... listen.

Find the worm.

FACING FURTHER INTO OUR HUNGER: THE EMPTY SELF AS A HUNGRY GHOST

To be rooted in true self we need to know the difference between the hunger of our true self and the hunger of our empty self. The basic difference is that our true self is keenly altruistic, motivated by a friendliness with the natural world. This friendliness presents itself as being able to ask ourselves such questions as: *What is this truly about?* This friendliness gives us an authentic and life-sustaining experience.

I took my walk one day as my daughter headed back to college after her first weekend home. It was a late October Sunday afternoon, sun low in the sky. I usually walk early in the morning. But I wanted to spend as much time as possible at home with my daughter. As I walked, I felt the hunger pangs of the empty self. Although some of it was grief and the late Sunday blues, there was a noticeable emptiness that begged to be filled. In my case, I noticed how strong my tendency was to fill up this sensation with thoughts of regret. I began to wonder what my life was going to look like now. I was sixty and my only child had left home to start her own life. How could I be excited about life the same way my daughter was about hers? What is the purpose of being old in this culture where age is looked down upon and even resented? Just the night before I had been asked if I wanted to use the senior discount at a local movie house where I attended a movie alone. He shouted out over the noisy, young, and coupled crowd. I took the financial advantage but felt the sting of looking old enough to be asked. As I walked, I realized I was nearing the end of my life while my daughter was at the start of hers. What I noticed most was my not wanting to feel this emptiness and how I searched for things to fill it.

This is what happens to most of us: the empty self is scared, hungry, hallow, and wounded and so begs to be filled. Then, if we are not attentive to our soul, our inner callings, we go about filling our emptiness in ways that become harmful to us and detrimental to the well-being of others. We over-consume, compete, demand to be recognized and applauded, con, lie, get aggressive, scapegoat and blame others, become addicted to drugs or alcohol or dependent on prescription medication, and as a result build a false self that is always hungry and searching for ways to keep this empty self filled.

We cannot stave off the empty self by ignoring it; it is always hungry. We can't feed it enough so that it becomes fulfilled and complete. Instead, our task is to hold a conversation with hunger, hang out with its many forms, and respond with our compassionate presence. I could have filled my emptiness by somehow "holding on" to my daughter, by drinking or overeating, by digressing into a state of regret and longing for the past, or by doing something else that would falsely feed the empty self and result in chronic hunger and disappointment. This hunger would then bring harm to both me and my daughter.

Our empty self feeds off of others and is tragically motivated by its sense of emptiness and fear, which is inherently self-absorbed and self-serving. We build a false self around this empty self so no one can truly know us—nor can we truly know ourselves. We are disconnected from reality. We become like a hungry ghost described in Buddhist narrative. The hungry ghost is a phantom that is chronically hungry and has a very small mouth. No matter how much it feeds itself, the "food" runs through it

> **There was that thought, most disturbing,**
> **that I wasn't enough.**
> **And before I could ask or answer for what?**
> **came the words** you'll never be able. **who?**
> **me? to what?**
> anything **the answer beat me again**
> **to the asking. And the more I chased that voice**
> **to find out whose it was,**
> **the deeper it retreated. Inward that is.**
> **And so it stays.**
> **But I have learned better**
> **than to whom it might belong. I have learned**
> **to answer those words**
> **with truths—most quieting.**

without being digested because, of course, ghosts don't have any way to process food. So they are always hungry, always eating, and never satisfied.

When we look into the nature of our hunger, we find that we are afraid of letting go of the hunger itself, believing we will never get what we want if we do. We fear that if we stop wanting this or craving that, we certainly won't ever get it. Our culture trains us to develop and pursue our hunger. Advertisements and various promotions push to keep us hungry because there is always more to have, more to do. And this reestablishes our fear that if we stop craving and grasping, we will stop getting. We grasp, hold on tight, and make demands while the empty self sends out its message of fear. The empty self focuses on what it does not have, or believes it does not have, and supports a chronic state of subtle anxiety. This hunger for something blocks the experience of receiving and increases our fear and hostility about not (seemingly) having it. We are unable or unwilling to ask ourselves *What is this really about* or to pause long enough to host any edges. This is much like being focused on the empty part of a cup that is half full and missing the fullness entirely. The thing is, the cup is always **both-and**: empty and full.

Of course, those who are trapped in the empty self syndrome cause others to suffer too. They project their hunger outside of themselves and blame outside circumstances and other people for what they lack. This further disempowers them in getting what they truly want. In this hungry state the world is seen as denying, frustrating, and negative. Those caught up in the empty self syndrome project hostility to the world around them. You can be president of the United States, but if you are a hungry ghost, even this won't satisfy your chronic need for approval.

In my Buddhist practices, the hungry ghost (empty self) is seen as feeding on the eight worldly concerns. These eight worldly concerns are: gain and loss, pleasure and pain, praise and blame, and fame and disgrace. We can become attached to gain, pleasure, praise, and fame, and do whatever we can to avoid loss, pain, blame, and disgrace. Of course, all these concerns are part of our human experience and can't be avoided entirely. At the same time, to be chronically hungry for gain, pleasure, praise, and fame means we perpetuate the empty self syndrome and stay in a chronic state of discontent and self-preservation.

Our true nature faces the empty self by being willing to do our inner work, to "be with" ourselves, to host the edges, to touch reality, and to continue to live our lives from the inside out with a firm hold on the red thread. This makes it possible to respond to our inner hunger in enriching ways. Always. Often with remarkable results.

Nothing outside of ourselves will ever bring us lasting happiness. Remember, *breathe and no effort*. Listen for the worm of true nourishment.

LETTING GO: AN INNER STATE OF SOLITUDE

Release from all our suffering has some component of letting go, which can be understood and experienced as an inner state of solitude. Living with the promise of paradox, we let go of the **either-or** mentality. Ultimately, we let go of a negative dynamic that drives our experience and relies on an antidote to guide us through our encounters. When we let go of always grasping at something or holding on to someone, in the moment of this release, we receive something greater. We let go of old stories and references and see the world anew. Letting go of "having to have something" opens us up to receiving what is truly available to us in the moment. This is the science of happiness and manifestation: we let go of searching and insisting on having one thing (the focusing illusion) and open up to the myriad of possibilities present in the moment. In our solitude and active contemplation, we let go of our "musts" and "have tos" and our fears that if we don't hold on to our search for happiness, happiness will not be found. In reality, happiness or serenity find us when we create a space of inner solitude for them. We make space by letting go.

The simple practice of naming what we want and then letting it go—not grasping or holding on tight, not turning our wants into "must haves"—will help us feed our real hunger in that we get what we truly want.

TRY THIS: A WAY TO LET GO

Start here. Name what you want—get specific, journal around it. For instance, *I want so and so to show me some appreciation; I want to be more abundant; I want to get the job; I want to have more serenity.* Be specific and clear with yourself. It's okay to want success and recognition. And it's better to admit it than have it go into hiding, become part of your shadow self, and seep out in negative ways. What will your success look like, be like, feel like when it is 100 percent true? The key is to be specific and honest with yourself.

This journaling is a way to name and bring forth what you want and then let it go and get on with living your life. In the Chinese Oracle of the I-Ching, this is identified as "Meeting the Creative Half-way." Instead of pushing ourselves to do it all, we leave room for the Creative to come and help us to fulfill our intentions. If we go past half-way and overdo, we don't leave room for the Creative to come in and offer help.

TRY THIS: THE POWER OF SCRIPTING

Scripting is a researched-based technique that is known to bring about positive results. In cognitive-behavioral therapies, scripting is a proven treatment for anxiety and fear. Both in Buddhist mind-training techniques and cognitive-behavioral practices, evidence reveals that what we hold in our minds directly influences our experiences. So in scripting, you create "scenes"—like you would in a movie script—of what you want or how you would like a particular event to unfold. You write these scenes out, by hand, in your journal. You write out what it will feel like, be like, look like in a particular future scene. You include how others will respond. So, this scene, in the writing of it and reviewing of it later, makes it more possible to get you what you want because you see it in your mind first. You recognize this particular desire as a possibility. You see the entire scene play out. This is contrary to what we too often do, which is to prepare for the worst or worry about how things are not going to work out for us.

After you have named your desire or/and scripted around it, let it go. When any wanting and grasping arises, yearning and hunger, drama or desperateness, let it go. Become aware of the emotions and then be willing to host them or let them go and be present for what is happening in the moment. Host the hunger. I simply say to myself, *I let this go*, and release the storyline and energy around what I crave. Think of it as making room for what you truly want through letting it go. The scripting is like sending a letter in and out—inward to your soul and outward to the world (or your Higher Power). Now let the letter go and be received and see what comes back to you.

Receive—not seek. A way to simplify this would be to say: *Don't waste more time searching for love, for happiness, for purpose; name what you want and then—let go. Don't be like the hungry boy who kept diving into the watery reflection of the pears he hungered for instead of noticing that the real pears were up in the tree, in his reach all along.* The mind, when in search mode, keeps us caught up in an illusion of what we think we have to have. It keeps us hungry and diving for illusions such as fame, gadgets, and "likes" on Facebook. The searching, grasping mind, especially when desperately or constantly looking for happiness or "our purpose," is sabotaged by the search itself. The boy can't let go of the illusion (reflection) of the pears. We can't let go of what we want in fear we will never get it. With others, when we let go, we no longer go about demanding what we want from them, for we have ceased to dwell on what we are not getting from them.

Become clear about what you want, name it, and script it, then in your letting go, make room for what can and will manifest. The reality (of the real pears) may be different from what you expect or want, but it will be real and life-giving.

A MOMENT OF SOLITUDE AND REFLECTION

In a time of silent reflection, check in with your inner self. What, based on your inner knowing and spiritual principles, will feed your hunger? What has fed your true self in the past? What is your true self asking for now? You may have already named it above: I want a job. But the empty self may be demanding something very specific that presents as wanting a certain job. Maybe what your soul is clamoring for is to be connected to others at work and content at your place of employment!

To let go and to open up you can always return to the state of exploration by being in the conversation about what you want. Live the question and remain, as best you can, in a place of receptivity, which is attained through non-clinging and letting go.

The master doesn't seek fulfiller.
Not seeking, not expecting,
She is present, and can welcome all things.

—Lao Tzu, *Tao Te Ching*

At some point our hunger will exhaust us if we are not feeding it what is life-giving. We may notice, too, that we are on our own. Only we can walk the **Inner Labyrinth**; no one can do our inner work for us. Furthermore, our efforts of self-improvement often go unnoticed by others. We will, of course, still benefit from such efforts. But typically, no one says, "Hey, Julie, I see that you are calmer, more centered and, oh! how hard you have worked at this!" So, at this time we tend to feel our aloneness and our solitude because we have been willing to slow down, do the inner work, and live our life from the inside out. We have faced our hunger. We often can't see how far we have come, how much peace and integrity we have gained. Another good reason for solitude!—we are graced with self-awareness. We recognize how rooted we are in true self.

TRUE, TRUER, TRUEST

I celebrate disappointments, for when I welcome them with an open mind, as the spiritual friend they are, I find they are openings to other possibilities, to something Spirit-handed. I trust disappointment and discouragement as a threshold and doorway to what wants to emerge. I wanted "this" but got "that."

This is true.

Truer yet is that something always waits on the other side of the threshold of disappointment, something that sustains the soul, something that moves our life forward.

Truest is that our faithfulness and perseverance will bring forth in our lives what we most want. Having not given up, we can feed well from the aquifers of true self through our faithfulness.

On my way out of my home to take a retreat to work on this book, I grabbed John O'Donohue's book *Anam Cara*, in which is found this quote: "In the neglected crevices and corners of your evaded solitude, you will find the treasure that you have always sought elsewhere."

> When I walked down the road
> taking only You,
> until the noise became less—and the light more true,
> then
> the river began to flow again
> under my skin.

CHAPTER FIVE

MEETING UP WITH THE MINOTAUR: FACING AND INTEGRATING SHADOW SELF

> *We must abandon the common sense notion that the monsters we meet within ourselves are enemies to be destroyed. Instead, we must cultivate the hope that they can become companions to be embraced, guides to be followed, albeit with caution and respect.*
>
> —Parker J. Palmer

Here we are at the center of our metaphorical labyrinth where we meet up with some part of ourselves we have resisted or ignored, where we obtain a realization that helps us become our best and truest selves. Confronting the Minotaur is about reaching a realization through our willingness to continue to go into our experiences. *We are not here to destroy the Minotaur as much as to integrate what he represents into our life. We have everything we need—as symbolized by our hold on the red thread—to turn the scary Minotaur into a spiritual friend. If we "kill" anything, it is his perceived ugliness, which represents a part of ourselves that we have not integrated, an unconscious, unwelcomed part of ourselves that is in agreement with some culturally endorsed illusion. This is an aspect of self that we sometimes, and to our peril, would rather ignore. It is the Minotaur who will devour us if we cannot accept and integrate this unconscious part of*

ourselves, or some part of the collective unconscious that we have come to agree with.

There always has been, and always will be, a shadow aspect to our experiences. So this heroic journey is one we can always be on; we can always keep hold of the red thread as we reach inward toward the center of ourselves.

I remind us here that in the overarching myth of the Minotaur and the Labyrinth, we are the superheroine. We are Theseus. We are the one who is willing to enter the labyrinth to do our inner work. We go into the labyrinth motivated by an altruistic intention to help others with a willingness to face what may have up to now been hidden from us. As discussed earlier but bears repeating here, the full story of Theseus, who we seek to emulate, fits the general pattern of a superhero: He was secretly fathered by a king, he performed heroic acts even as a child, he won the love of Ariadne, he descended into the labyrinth to benefit others, and he successfully "killed" the Minotaur.

However, later in life he got a big head and believed he was the biggest and the best! He then confronted another shadow in the form of Hades.

These challenges that Theseus faced as he grappled with his ego remind us that through life and myth, we cannot separate ourselves from our own shadow.

In some versions of the myth of the red thread, Ariadne gave Theseus a sword with which to kill the Minotaur. In Buddhist mythology and symbolism, swords and knives are used to "cut through" illusion and give way to our true nature. In Hindu mythology, the Minotaur could be understood as Kali, the goddess of transformation. She holds the archetypal power to help us let go of our illusions and projections. She, too, is a frightening creature. Kali wears a necklace of severed heads and a skirt of severed arms. The heads are smiling because they have been freed from their illusions and from the negative influences of the ego (their hungry ghost).

As we make the journey to the center of the labyrinth—our own center—parts of us will not survive the journey, nor should they. Aspects of our ego must be sacrificed and released for us to be able to turn around and take the journey outward as authentic and reliable leaders and citizens.

The Minotaur may be understood as a Thunder Being—a creature who basically scares the truth out of us! Thunder Beings are the central archetypes of transformation that reside in the psyche and come out in the form of gods and goddesses and methods to free us from our egos and our more unconscious shadow aspects. In this case, the Thunder Being waits for us at the center of an inward journey and is always central to understanding oneself. We must routinely integrate this part of our hidden self before we are ready to move onward and serve others. Oftentimes, this encounter is a major turning point in our life, a deal breaker, a place of realization and assimilation. You will know when you are there because there is no going forward in the same old way.

Only with the puissant forces needed to break through the illusions can we release more of our inner nature. To see this in another way, imagine your true nature is being held captive by beasts that represent such dynamics as taking sides; being competitive; feeling shame or chronic regret; and/or feeling indifference, isolation, or apathy. An equally powerful energy must help you destroy their grip. However, it is often the case that when these demons show up, our patterned response to difficulty often tugs on us, pulling us into habitual ways of dealing with the life issues being presented.

The thunder energy that we need in response at this point may be found in various spiritual practices around the world. In Christianity, Thunder symbolizes the voice of God as a divine threat of annihilation or revelation. (Job 36:29–33) And in the ancient Chinese oracle of the *I Ching*, the attribute of Thunder (Zhen) is movement. The Thunder Being of Islam is named Jibrail, the giver of revelation. Some deals with the ego (false self) die here. Transformative death is a letting go of such illusions as arrogance, indifference, judgment, entitlement, and superiority. We are freed of some illusion that the collective shadow perpetuates. These illusions, these dynamics that we agree to, as Parker reminded me, "can keep us in our place." We can be fooled into complacency and silence. We then would give up at the moment we should step forward.

Only through the inner journey can we understand that there is always a dance present between the dark and the light. I share the understanding with Parker that the best teachers, leaders, and friends—as well as places in our own being—are both wound and antidote, illusion and reality, shadow and light. If we expect to live honestly and wholly, we can't have one without the other. This is a great and often hidden paradox, a most beneficent **both-and**: shadow and light are always together, side-by-side. Those who ignore or deny the shadow are a danger to themselves and others. Those who set out to eradicate their imperfections and darkness are in denial of their basic humanity. That's one reason I challenge views of enlightenment where someone claims there is no shadow, no ego. I've distanced myself from a few false spiritual and psychological gurus who claim they have beat the ego. Follower beware! There lies the darkest ego, hidden behind this false claim to light. We can all touch reality, but that only means we were able to integrate the dark or use the dark to touch the light at a particular time.

We are always both, but we tend to keep the unlikeable parts of ourselves unconscious and in the dark. However, these places are where, in most myths, the treasures are also kept—deep in that same dark cave. We discover that in our pilgrimage inward, to the cave where the treasures lie, there are many bones left at the foot of the beast. They are only inches away from the riches. The message they impart is: Don't give in to resistance or fear. Don't become the heap of bones a few feet from the treasures. Knowing a treasure is waiting for us at the end of our explorations can serve to motivate us to keep moving through the discomfort and pain we must endure in the dark of the cave, in the dark nights of the soul and our encounters with our Minotaur.

Sometimes, however, we want to be happy or enlightened so badly that we deny the more shadowy aspects of ourselves. We repress the idea that we aren't as kind or as evolved as we would like to believe we are. Or we believe the shame and feel there is something fundamentally wrong with us. We think we have our ego in check (or our shit together). We come to believe that one slaying of the Minotaur means we are done. Or we forget that we are, after all, human with superpowers, and that having limits—and an ego—is part of our humanity.

THE PARADOXICAL NATURE OF THE MINOTAUR

The Minotaur itself represents the bringing together of opposites. It is a symbol of our inherent paradoxical nature, the meeting of opposites or *coincidentia oppositorum*. As such it is the **both-and** of beast and human, rational and irrational, spiritual and habitual, deity and demon, good and evil, illusion and reality.

For me the Minotaur holds two key paradoxical aspects. One is that we hide goodness in our shadow. At some point and for some reason, we were discouraged from showing our most heroic and truest selves, our most vulnerable selves. We were told to not brag or not to "show off" when we were simply showing ourselves. We were simply declaring through an outward act of vulnerability, "Hey, look, I can do this!" while adults around us shunned or even belittled us. Any childhood trauma affects our ability to feel our inner light. When our loveliness is not mirrored back to us, we often forget we have it.

I don't agree with Marianne Williamson (though I appreciate her work) who famously speaks in a poem how it often is our greatness, our capabilities that most frighten us and that we work to keep hidden from ourselves. Not so! We haven't learned how to let it all out. We hold the capacity and even inherent desire to be vulnerable in this way, but we forget how to brag and show off. We are held back by how we perceive ourselves or believe others perceive us, and we have come to feel unsafe in our vulnerabilities of exposing ourselves in this way. We may have forgotten how to reveal these qualities. So this is more about feeling safe in our vulnerabilities than being scared to show our light.

When we don't claim our greatest assets—our compassion or creative expression—we tend to let others in positions of authority tell us who and what we are and what we want. This is such a great loss, a waste for the individual and for the world.

The second paradoxical twist to the archetype of the Minotaur is that when we face our illusions and integrate some aspect of our unconscious, we release him from his prison. The truth is, given that the Minotaur represents embodied values and, as such, is a cultural construct, someone else created the Minotaur. This further represents how we came to believe certain things about ourselves and the world that simply are not true. We have become imprisoned by the illusions made by "mad" men, angry people, those who don't want their privilege challenged, who want to control and manipulate us, people who don't want us to show our inner light because they feel it may outshine theirs. But when we do speak our truth or take a seat at the table, we free them as well.

TAKING YOUR SEAT AT THE TABLE

Facing and integrating the Minotaur—our hidden demons—is essential to our individual and collective humanity. Those who want to unnerve or keep us from getting a seat at the table use fear and manipulation to do so. And they can't manipulate someone who knows who they are, who is comfortable in their vulnerabilities.

So if someone tells me, "You're not smart enough, Julie," in an attempt to undermine me, I am not triggered into inaction or hopelessness because I know who I am. When someone insults me, I think: *tell me something I don't know. I have felt stupid at times, but I have not hidden the fear of being discovered as stupid in my shadow. So, yes, tell me something I don't know about myself!* And then I take my seat at the table.

When we keep our light hidden because the shadow tells us to do so—*don't brag, don't shine too bright*—this sets us up to be controlled and manipulated. Here is where the bully gaslights and inhibits us when we don't integrate our shadow self, that shadow self that hides our vulnerabilities and light.

I was recently bullied by someone who hid behind the disguise of a nice, talented guy I met when I first arrived in my new community. The details of the story and of him are not important because for each of us the details are unique but the bullying is universal. Overtime I felt increasingly inferior after our encounters. I call this "that shrinking experience"—when being with someone makes you shrink somehow. So I knew it was time to enter the **Inner Labyrinth** and explore these encounters. As I trusted my experience (the second turn in the **Inner Labyrinth**) and quickly understood what I experienced (I was being bullied), I moved into transformation, and I sought closure with him. In response, he kept trying to bully me into another conversation where he would once again try to prove himself. In his final text to me, he mentioned how

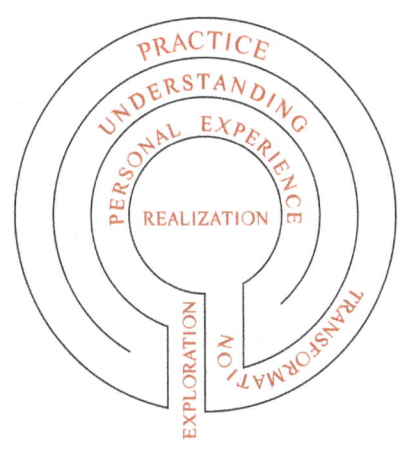

we should talk because "I don't want either of us to feel awkward when we encounter each other." This was an attempt to force a certain narrative on me. I then moved into the Realization part of the **Inner Labyrinth** where my clarity reassured me to act on my knowing. I had arrived at a realization that included not having any need to engage anymore. I did later respond to his text to let him know that "I am okay with being awkward."

In revealing our illusions, the Minotaur also reveals some of our greatest gifts. And each gift, each realization is a coming together of opposites; it's a transformation of contradiction into paradox. And as we meet up with our outer and inner bullies—the shadowy aspects of self and others—we can rely on the **Inner Labyrinth** again and again to lead us naturally to a realization. As Francis of Assisi said: "There are beautiful, wild forces within us. Let them turn the mills inside and fill sacks that feed even heaven."

PUTTING THE SHADOW IN SERVICE OF THE LIGHT

THE MINOTAUR OF SHAME

Any of us who have experienced any kind of trauma—abandonment; verbal, emotional, sexual, or spiritual abuse; neglect; alcoholism or mental illness of a parent—will meet up with the Minotaur of Shame. Shame is always threaded to some painful experience you endured at the hands of others and have come to internalize. The beauty is that when you meet up with shame, its paradoxical nature is revealed and you discover that you have nothing to be ashamed of! This shame points to a wound that is now ready to be healed.

It finally came—that knock on my door. I knew it would. I was found out. Caught. It was a Saturday morning back in the early 1990s, and the mailman brought a note saying that the post office had a certified letter for me, but I would have to go sign for it. The unexpected knock itself triggered shame—who besides an unhappy visitor with bad news would be knocking on my door? And the unknown contents of the certified letter only strengthened the shame. I was in some big trouble for something. But I couldn't pinpoint what caused these feelings. Where did this feeling of shame come from? What would cause me to hold a negative assumption about an unexpected knock at the door? I couldn't connect it to anything I recalled ever doing.

The Minotaur of Shame is a feeling that something is fundamentally wrong, even though we can't always connect it to something. What is the meaning of those dreams we have in which we didn't take enough college credits to get our diploma, and so "they" would soon hunt us down and get their credentials back? What makes us feel bad about ourselves when we are actually doing well? The shadow of shame is jealous, possessive, and deceitful. It will ruin your life if you let it.

We don't have to figure out how or why we feel shame; suffice it to say it derives from some past trauma. And do not confuse shame with guilt. Guilt takes on the flavor of feeling accountable about something you did or experienced, like accidentally hitting an animal with your car because you were driving too fast, or getting angry with your child because you were having a bad day. Similar to the difference between hurt and pain, guilt (like pain) results in some transformative effort on your part, while shame (like hurt) mires you down. Instead of getting caught up in the why of it all, work with the energy of shame itself. Shame is corrosive if not brought to light. Understand that you have personalized a negative, oftentimes traumatic past experience. If there are no words or explanations for your feelings of shame, the incidences may have occurred before you could speak—so there are no words for it. And understand that both children and adults tend to personalize abuse. When this happens, the shame tends to go underground (into the shadow) and surfaces to interfere with the natural state of joy and connection.

This knock on my door, which occurred over twenty-five years ago, helped me become aware of the shame I carried within me and how easily it was triggered. I took this as the entryway into my true inheritance of happiness and belonging and began to release the bonds of shame. Fortunately, we don't need to know the specifics of the original causes to heal or transform from shame. Instead of holding shameful thoughts and acting from this place, we can name shame, bring it to the light, and identify its antidote. Again, we can work on what holds us back—trauma in our everyday lives and present-day experiences. We don't have to focus on our past. That knock on the door brought my shame to light. Then, on Monday, I discovered what the letter actually contained. The bank was letting me know that my security box payment was due. Ha!

The repressed or denied collective shadow can strip us of our humanity. We unconsciously act out the more repressed aspects of this collective shadow and find ourselves hypnotized by the communal movement around us. On the flip side, when we are seen as standing alone in our truth, often the collective shadow's response is to view us as wrong, crazy, or not worth listening to. Objectification of others comes from an agreement with the collective shadow. When making "the other" wrong, we dehumanize them. And the need for us to be in agreement with some collective assumption dehumanizes us.

Additionally, the collective shadow can be felt as the current we swim against. Others may not want us to do our inner work to meet our shadow because they are afraid of facing their own.

Our families also have strong, influential agreements that, when we individuate, enable us to be met with the some response that tries to keep us in agreement with the family's shadow. When I spoke of my worries about a brother's addiction, I was shamed and quieted by being told I was "too sensitive." I was often told to "lighten up," which I find to be humorous now since that is exactly what I was attempting to do: bring light to some darkness.

To move against a collective shadow is truly a heroine's journey. Theseus went against his father and king to stop the slaughter of innocents. A commitment to remain aware and remember we always have blind spots means to keep the shadow in view.

A shadow element that causes harm is the need to take sides (a cousin to the need to be right). This suppressed shadow makes others our enemies. The continued repression of the shadow is what results in situations like Nazi Germany. We are pushed to take sides in elections, in our disagreements, in war, in debates, in fights, in family conversations. Finding it hard to work, play, or disagree without taking sides points to how deep-seated the construct of "taking sides" is in our collective shadow. I have shared how this dynamic rose up in my more recent explorations. And this dynamic rose out of my unconscious; I thought I was "done with all that." But this is such a deeply rooted, culturally endorsed dynamic that we all have this contradiction inside us, and we continually encounter it in our work and our efforts in the world.

It is also worth noting that even spiritual groups—such as sanghas, retreats, religious gatherings, and even circles of trust—hold a collective shadow. No group is exempt. The more dangerous groups either keep the shadow in the unconscious or intentionally use it to manipulate others. In groups, acknowledging our agreements is essential. Basically, as Carl Jung warns us: "Until you make the unconscious conscious, it will direct your life and you will call it fate."

Today our cultural inheritance includes the Internet. The Internet, with its constant contact, is an accepted, even expected, part of our daily lives. I find that we can hide in the shadows of our postings, behind Facebook profiles and pictures that make life appear so even and perfect, or overly dramatic. We can "like" this and that without even holding a conversation with anyone. We can argue a cause online but not take any real action for change. For me, this adds to our keeping things unconscious and in the dark because anything that separates us from true conversation with our own hearts and the hearts of others is more hindrance than gain. We have come to falsely believe we are making a difference when we are not. The Internet needs to be a tool for leaders and change agents but should not take the place of face-to-face conversation, community building, and real-life civil disobedience. We are becoming a culture whose shadow of indifference may be what kills us off. And at the root of our indifference is agreeing to not make a difference.

For certain, given all of the technology present in our world, taking reflective breaks to contemplate our lives is becoming increasingly difficult to do. But we must. And as compassionate citizens, we must show others the way to face the darkness and the wounds of the world so we can be active in embracing our lives out in the world in true conversation.

THE SHADOW OF INDIFFERENCE (OR KILLING OFF THE OTHER)

Our explorations and discoveries around our dynamics is all shadow work. It's putting our shadow in service of the light. We put the shadow of shame in service of the light through our realization that we internalized someone else's abuse.

To face our darkness means to be in the dark, to experience the dark but not be consumed by it. This facing means to open our hearts to ourselves first, so we can then open our hearts to others. The first half of our journey through this book represents doing our inner work so we can do our outer work—out there. We will have healing powers available to us because we have healed some of what is broken inside ourselves.

Indifference is a way to kill off "the other" in our hearts and minds. Indifference renders the other as irrelevant. I learned in my youth to use indifference as a way to protect and defend myself. In my indifference, I could walk away without having revealed myself to those who were out to control or sought to destroy me; I could walk away without having risked anything, and I could shut out the pain around me. While it may have protected me in some lethal situations, having indifference as a habitual response held me back from true intimacy. Indifference prevented me from truly exploring places and people, and even the internal landscape of my own heart and mind. It made me less vulnerable and available, and, therefore, of less benefit to others. Indifference robbed me of my healing powers. I was not able to make a difference. And when I became indifferent to another, I lost my sense of responsibility to them or to their story. Anytime I find myself wanting to turn away from another, act like what they say doesn't matter, or shut myself off from them in some way, I do my best to face my indifference—and quickly.

Have you ever relied on indifference to navigate a challenging encounter or dark time in your life? Have others bumped up against this wall, this indifference in you? Have you hit an interior place of indifference? Indifference has the power to devour our light if we are not careful. I believe that a misuse of drugs, therapies, alcohol, overeating, time on the Internet, and other pastimes can be used to "make us indifferent." These can distract us from wanting to make a difference.

A casual, dispassionate response to life's circumstances becomes, even if unwittingly, a defense that prevents us from taking responsibility for our experiences. Indifference used as a method of protection shuts us down, and we can no longer receive from or give to another. This apathy can show up in relationship to ourselves and to our choices. We may claim that this choice, this action doesn't matter, but in reality every choice plays a significant part in future conditions and experiences.

Eleanor Roosevelt warned, "One day we will destroy the moon with indifference."

THE ANTIDOTE TO INDIFFERENCE: VULNERABILITY

An antidote to indifference can be vulnerability, a vulnerable curiosity and receptivity to ourselves and others. We can develop an appreciation for the other, whether the other is an individual or a situation. In fact, all antidotes to our negative dynamics challenge our indifference and make us vulnerable. When we let a dynamic like indifference or being judgmental guide our experience, we are letting our shadow direct the experience. When we bring forth our antidote of love or courage, we are being vulnerable with ourselves and others.

Vulnerability is another superpower.

Through our vulnerability we are known to ourselves and we become known to others. All our dynamics, which are also shadow aspects of ourselves, thrive in the dark, build in strength in secrecy. Brought to the light, a process itself that makes us vulnerable, we become able to receive such antidotes as forgiveness, love, and belonging.

This place of vulnerability is also where we make contact with one another and where the eternal conversation takes place. Our vulnerability is our truth and is us being fearless.

Through this journey inward and out, we do not destroy

the shadow, we hold a conversation with it. And through this conversation we bring our love, joy, and belonging to the light.

TEACHING STORY: CHALLENGING OUR INDIFFERENCE

There is a story of a young man who thought it wouldn't matter if he littered just once, so he dropped a plastic bag off the side of his boat. When he did so, a fish got caught in it. An eagle, seeing the struggling fish, swooped down to catch the fish to feed its three young offspring waiting in their nest along the riverbank. The eagle began to choke on the plastic and flew in front of a car, which caused the car to swerve. The car hit a vehicle coming from the other direction and both drivers were killed. The eagle died alongside the road.

Every action, no matter how small, causes yet another action; there is always a chain of events resulting from any simple action. A dramatization of a far more lethal result from such small "litterings" is this: Plastic pollution has a direct and deadly effect on wildlife and their habitats. Thousands of seabirds and sea turtles, seals, and other marine mammals are killed each year after ingesting plastic or getting entangled in it. Endangered wildlife like Hawaiian monk seals and Pacific loggerhead sea turtles are among nearly three hundred species that eat and get caught in plastic litter. There are now many large "dead zones" both in the ocean and on land due to the way and the speed with which we are polluting our environment.

CONTEMPLATIVE BREAK

We can meditate on the possible chain of events that may take place from such small personal decisions and actions. Consider some small decision you are making now and what the resulting link of events may be. Focus on something that has some shadow quality to it, like keeping a secret, or gossiping about someone, or telling a "little lie."

Now imagine the young man in the above story choosing not to litter. Watch the story unfold as he goes home to his son, who is in third grade, and asks him to put the bag in the recycling bin. The son mentions that they are learning about recycling in their class at school. And the father says, "Yes, my father taught me to leave a place better then you found it." There are now good feelings all around.

We use indifference to back away from something we would do much better getting into. We use our indifference as a shield against our vulnerabilities.

Engage or withdraw? That is the question.

PUTTING INDIFFERENCE IN THE SERVICE OF THE LIGHT

Bringing our indifference to the service of the light means first and last taking 100 percent responsibility for our experiences, facing into what arises in our life, not away. In this we take responsibility for our inner struggles instead of blaming others or outside circumstances. Once again, everything becomes material to be present with rather than evade. We don't pass the buck or shut down because in so doing we also forfeit the power to change events, to make a difference. We can face into times we sense ourselves shutting down or pulling away. We can stay with our experience and ask: *What small difference can I make?* We can engage the Three R's where we become receptive to reality by asking: *What is this really about?*

As I share in my book *The Zero Point Agreement,* this is how we "live life from our side," from the inside out.

This approach makes us responsive rather than reactive, makes us the cause of our life rather than the effect. Once we bring some light to indifference by claiming responsibility for our experiences, we automatically make a difference. We may not see the impacts of our engagement, but they are there.

Facing into our indifference is a way to host the edges of others. We can learn to be present for others' edges (page 162) and not have to do a deep dive into indifference when confronted with our own or another's suffering.

One of the greatest results of doing this inner work is that whether a life situation is wonderful or not depends on how our mind perceives it and relates to it. How we interpret events in our life is determined wholly by inner conditions. His Holiness the Dalai Lama shares with us that having worried thoughts doesn't change the outcome. You worry and something bad happens; the worrying didn't stop it. You worry and something works out well; all the worrying was a waste of energy.

Indifference can be just a small quiet turning away when what we should do is turn toward, like I did in the above encounter with a bully. I could have turned away in indifference.

"YOU STILL HAVE A FEW BLIND SPOTS"

"Julie, you still have a few blind spots," a spiritual teacher reminded me during our last time together. I was leaving Minneapolis to move down to Spring Green, Wisconsin. She didn't, of course, tell me what these blind spots were; it was a gentle reminder that I still had them. I had done a lot of inner work up until that time. So it's safe to assume that I may have gotten a bit arrogant around my efforts and growth. I could have become like Theseus after his successes with the Minotaur; he thought of himself as infallible and as the greatest king ever. He had forgotten he still had blind spots. We all have blind spots. It's not the blind spots that get us in trouble as much as it is forgetting we have them. Now when I am having difficulty, I remind myself that chances are I'm encountering another blind spot.

WON'T WE ALL . . . DON'T WE ALL?

Sometimes when we've come this far "in" and have done some great inner work, we may assume there can't be more. But using this metaphor of the encounter with the Minotaur, notice that it is on the journey inward, right before we face out and do our work in the world that we are apt to confront a shadow aspect, a blind spot.

When we own our shadow self and acknowledge that we have weaknesses and blind spots, we kill the beastly part of the Minotaur. Put another way, which is how I see this archetype, when we meet him face to face, he won't destroy us.

I want to mention here that as an author, I often find a

"writer's" blind spot within myself and other authors. When we writers are honest with ourselves and our readers, we will admit that it is through our writing that we figure things out. Getting published doesn't in any way mean our inner work is done. Bestselling authors, in particular, are in danger of believing that we are special and above the rest. No. We who write, teach, and lead others are prone to more blind spots than those who are less public with their acts. Popularity and fame can be intoxicating, and a culturally endorsed illusion is that fame feeds the soul. However, it doesn't. Fame only encourages the empty self, as shown in the previous chapter.

> There's no Joy in those old halls,
> where the heap rises, falls or fades,
> and the next *same* takes its place.
> Though once bright with youthful choosings, Joy's exceptional face was forgotten
> long ago, given over to conformity,
> then certainty.

A CONTEMPLATIVE MOMENT: BREATHE INTO IT

Let's take a break and breathe, find a contemplative moment, and admit we still have blind spots. There is still "stuff" hiding in our unconscious.

As heroines in our own story, we commit to continuing to acknowledge our blind spots. The greatest difference I witness right now in our leaders is between those who wear their humanity on their sleeve by owning their limits and blind spots, and those who don't. Such unconscious aspects as fear, greed, arrogance, and power drive those who don't claim their blind spots. They are the hungry ghosts among us. And they are in a position to project all their wounds, their shadowy illusions onto the world. So the next time you are up against a challenge, take a breath, acknowledge that you have blind spots, and be willing to explore what they might be. Be willing to enter the **Inner Labyrinth**. Just a simple opening to explore a simple acknowledgment is enough to soften your stance on the outside and bring that inner relief and awareness that leads to a personal realization.

> You have to go more than once to that place,
> before it is truly familiar,
> before you then know how to grace—
> fully leave it behind.

BECOMING OUR OWN

On a visit with my elderly mother, I witnessed another lesson in indifference. In the independent living center where she resides, the residents have dinner together in a community room. These dinners are an opportunity to engage in conversation, to hear differing points of view, and maybe, just maybe, to be mutually influenced. Sadly, in her way (common to those of her generation), my mother said, "I made everyone promise not to bring up politics or religion!" In this she was unwilling to confront the shadow self. Instead she was very proud of setting this rule at the table, whereas I was saddened that this opportunity to make a constructive difference, even if ever so small, was passed up. After all, they are all still alive and most are registered voters. If nothing else, we can learn to listen to the other and be moved by them, even if it feels a bit awkward and we are unnerved by our differences. To keep the shadow out of our stories and conversations, even at such a late point in our lives, means we have given up on the other and on ourselves.

In the end, we can only be with others in the way we can be with ourselves. As Ralph Waldo Emerson said: "We must be our own before we can be another's." I am good with awkward. You?

We have, through our continued inner journey, become our own. We know more about who we are and what we are capable of. Now we can become another's in community and vocation, as the leaders and citizens we know ourselves to be.

And, Dear Reader, you too still have blind spots.

That chill brush of you, even slight,
says I can't leave you—try as I may,
skulking back
around however many corners of my mind.

But today I turned the chase,
looked me dead in the eye, and saw you more
clearly. Lending your strengths too,
dark as they are,
in the broken places, alongside the lauded light;
when I need you, maybe I'll call—maybe ally,
now that I know your name.

CHAPTER SIX

THE RETURN JOURNEY: AT THE THRESHOLD OF EXPERIENCE

Truth evolves within us, between us, and around us as we participate in the 'eternal conversation.' My working definition of truth is simple, though practicing it is anything but: 'Truth is an eternal conversation about things that matter, conducted with passion and discipline.' Truth cannot possibly be found in the conclusions of the conversation, because the conclusions keep changing. So if we want to 'live in truth,' it is not enough to live in the conclusions of the moment. We must find a way to live in the continuing conversation, with all its conflicts and complexities, while staying in close touch with our own inner teacher.

—Parker J. Palmer

Each new experience that awakens in you adds to your soul and deepens your memory. The person is always a nomad, journeying from threshold to threshold, into ever different experiences.

—John O'Donohue

Here we reach a threshold in our lives: a place where we have encountered or explored something deeply personal. We have come to a time when we will either stay put and not move forward based on our new awareness, or we will cross this threshold between what was and what is yet to become. ***The active life is full of thresholds.*** Just so, nature, the cycle of day into night and night back into day, offers thresholds and places for us to make contact and to hold an eternal conversation.

Here at some threshold you have touched something divine in yourself by embracing a shadow element. Emerson said, "No one suspects the days to be Gods." But they can be. This points to a core realization that I now carry through my life: ***our everyday life is the temple of our awakening.*** We don't need to go anywhere special. Special is here in our day-to-day lives and begins with each threshold of each new day. This particular threshold, this place where you find yourself now is where you will meet up with the divine. ***Thresholds are a place of renewal, release, and breakthrough. Every contradiction turned paradox is a threshold.***

There are liminal thresholds, internal thresholds, primal and spiritual thresholds, physical and seasonal thresholds where light and dark come together, where often a sacred contradiction gives us no other choice than to turn our back at what is finished and face out and forward to what is to come.

Arriving here means we have come to many internal thresholds of contemplation and action. Our book's poet, Rebecca Cecchini, as with all great poets, brings us to many thresholds of imagination and language, experience and language. Finding words where there are none to be found is a threshold. Leaving a marriage, entering a relationship, changing your mind are all thresholds, until we reach the final threshold between here and the Great Unknown.

THE GIFT OF THRESHOLD: THE GREAT CONVERSATION

Poet William Stafford was the perfect embodiment of a person living a life from the inside out through his words and through contemplation and solitude while otherwise living an active life in the larger community. I was introduced to the Threshold of the Great Conversation through William Stafford's work. His journey with words began most mornings before sunrise. A

Find a Way

What takes us out into the wilds but our own desires?

The hill begs climbing.
Your reluctant feet, so fearful of tangles,
cannot stand still for the singing on the slope.
Sun-lifted grasses promise your heart the same lightness.
So you go.

From afar you didn't see the path.
But naturally you accept its welcome.

Those whose feet moved through,
leaving only the open setting for their tales of
coming and going,
are nowhere in sight.

Left now in the quiet space, for the harvest
of your imagination, is every possible beginning
and ending of the travels;
a tale of your own creating—from a desire
that grew to be your finding of a way
unexpected.

conscientious objector during World War II, an unswerving ritual of his was to set pen to paper every day before dawn. Stafford's ritual of getting up before the sun is a thread we can all take hold of, if we so choose. At this threshold between night and day, we can tap into a universal language, one that is not bound by dogma or beliefs; we can tap into the vibrations and intentions of an awakening world. In so doing, we can set the tone for a day of living life from our side of the conversation, like the threshold we are at now, having reached the center of our labyrinth where we face outward to begin a return journey to a new home.

Whether it be with an idea, ourselves, others, nature, or a Higher Power, being engaged with what is present at the moment means we are moving from threshold to threshold, experiencing the dynamic conversational nature of life. Our suffering is a conversational threshold with what will heal us. Just like our conversation with our dynamic gave way to our antidote, our conversation with what is present reveals a threshold to us. **Like change, thresholds are a constant.**

THE GREAT UNKNOWN: AN ALWAYS PRESENT THRESHOLD

My spiritual pilgrimage began at a very young age as I searched for a sense of place and belonging. The Lutheran minister who, when I was eight, told the story of the monk on the cliff and later baptized me with "just" tap water at thirteen was my first spiritual teacher. His stories and support encouraged me to keep looking within for the meaning and belonging I craved. During the younger years of my pilgrimage, I was a vigilante in search of God. Later in life, I found that giving up the myth of the spiritual quest was a way to "discover Spirit" in my day-to-day experiences. On my path to the present, I found the *I Ching* at the age of sixteen. I also began to refer to God as the Great Unknown. This helped me hold a conversation with that "Something" I knew was here without holding it captive in some religious scheme.

Then, not too long ago, I had a dark passage that lasted about two years wherein I felt a break in my connection to Spirit, although I didn't give up my various spiritual practices entirely. I had been heartbroken by the dogma and possessiveness within a spiritual sangha where I had previously, for years, found teachings and refuge. What broke my relationship with these teachers and teachings was my inability to endorse their emphasis on ritual, their belief in and manipulation of the idea of hell, their advocacy of human dominion over the Earth, and their emphasis on accumulating merit through certain rigid practices.

At one particular dark edge, I felt desperate and wanted to give up. I can't say how that "giving up" would have manifested entirely, but I felt a bottom to my hope, which I'd never felt before. My connection to the teachings and to my spiritual source felt severed. I did manage to keep some conversation going with the

Great Unknown, although I had more or less given up on the idea that God, or some greater power, existed.

My isolation from spiritual friends and from my spiritual source generated a chronic sadness in me. Was I utterly on my own? Determined to lift myself out of my malaise, I went online and looked at an email I'd received from Wisdom Publications on their recent books. There was one book written by His Holiness the Dalai Lama, so I though it would be relatively user-friendly. His teachings were generous, and more often than not they were nondogmatic. So I clicked on "purchase" and waited for the book to arrive. I had a small ligament of hope as well as the intention of using the book's teachings as a way to host this particular edge and hopefully get beyond it.

When the book arrived, I dove into it within minutes and couldn't believe what I was reading! This from the foreword by Donald Swearer: "It is only by being in nature that the trees, rocks, earth, sand, animals, birds, and insects can teach us the lesson of forgetting the self—being at one with the Dharma. The destruction of nature, then, implies the destruction of Dharma."

I can now reveal that some of the disillusionment I felt with my former colleagues at the sangha was due to their belief that animals, although sentient beings, are less than we are. We are considered the better species, as taught in so many religions. This assumption encourages a selfishness that is wholly destructive. I felt then and continue to believe now that we are all part of a great circle of life.

Further in the foreword by Donald Swearer, I read how it is important for us to live "according to the laws of nature, and the consequences of following the laws of nature reflect his view that all human beings share a common natural environment and are part of communities embedded in the natural order of things. This interconnected universe we inhabit is the natural condition of things. To act contrary to this law of nature is to suffer because such actions contradict reality. Consequently, the good of the individual parts is predicated on the good of the whole, and vice versa."

These words spoke directly to my recent alienation from my sangha. On nearly every visit I had made to the temple, a nun had pointed out various things I was doing incorrectly. The emphasis in the book that I held in my hands wasn't on ritual and worship and doing things correctly, but on understanding our part in the natural scheme of things and respecting the interconnectedness of reality.

Jack Kornfield wrote in his preface: "When I asked him how so many Westerners who begin spiritual life with deep inner wounds, pain, and self-hatred can best approach practice, he replied simply with two suggestions. First, their whole spiritual practice should be enveloped by the principles of metta (loving kindness). Then they should be taken out into nature, into beautiful forests or mountains. They must stay there long enough to realize that they too are a part of nature."

I wept and felt the active, large conversation between me and the Great Unknown. I felt myself at a threshold.

But I wondered.

I was getting through the forward and preface with no mention of His Holiness the Dalai Lama and only occasional references to Buddhadasa Bhikkhu. I read on and when I got into the text it became clear to me that the book I had received was not the one I'd ordered. The cover of the book was the one I'd ordered, but the book inside the cover was not. The publisher or printer had mistakenly put this book inside the Dalai Lama's book cover.

The book I ordered was *The Middle Way: Faith Grounded in Reason*, by the Dalai Lama, translated by Thupten Jinpa. The title of the book I received was *The Heartwood of the Bodhi Tree: The Buddha's Teaching on Voidness* by Buddhadasa Bhikkhu, edited by Santikaro Bhikkhu. At the time, I would not have chosen a book about voidness. I already felt enough void and was drawn, as I shared earlier, to teachings from His Holiness the Dalai Lama. And yet, this book that I'd received instead was exactly what my soul needed at that time. This book and its message instantly lifted me out of my darkness. This is because I knew at the time I was being helped.

Early on in the book, I read: "To call something a 'fundamental principle of Buddhism' is only correct if, first, it is a principle that aims at the quenching of *dukkha* (pain, misery, suffering) and, second, it has a logic that one can see for oneself without having to believe others." Buddhadasa Bhikkhu warns here about spiritual life becoming a matter of "superstition, or rites and

> **It always bothered you that you couldn't see
> from where your strength might arise.**
>
> **But even now, having been you,
> I won't say. No,**
>
> **I smile at the remembrance of your (now)
> unsettled soul.**
>
> **For if not for that
> steaming, impatient, sometimes bitter brew
> of knowing and not knowing inside you,
> I might have settled - a tourist
> on the one trip I was given to lead.**
>
> **But, from this grand view of where you are headed,
> I can offer one small sweetening: knowing
> (as already you must)
> you will always be met.**

rituals, and of making merit by rote to insure against some kind of fear; [where then] there is no contact with real Buddhism." This was exactly what I needed to read and to receive to host the edge of my spiritual discontent and isolation. I read through the book, taking in its message as my heart opened up at this threshold to a revitalized conversation with the Great Unknown.

Further into the book, I learned that its transcriber and teacher, Santikaro, who had previously been living in Thailand, was now living only an hour's drive away from me in Wisconsin. There he and his spouse had established a quiet rural refuge center (Kevela Retreat Center). I have since attended some of his teachings and will continue to do so.

What made the Unknown known to me was remaining at this threshold and conversing with its inherent edge. If I had given up on this conversation at this dark time, I cannot be sure where I would be now. And I so love the contradictions and paradoxical nature of the Great Unknown's arrival coming to me in Buddhist teachings that I can understand and relate to.

As long as we keep the conversation going and keep hold of the red thread, the Great Unknown in return becomes a thread and the giver of threads.

This practice of staying in the eternal conversation with the Great Unknown is not always easy, but as I do, when I do, I feel myself to be an expression of this great source. Other large conversations on this same order of magnitude can take place while we sit under a tree, walk mindfully on a path, or sit somewhere in the wild at a time the sun is about to rise or set. These thresholds of conversation hold the secret nectar of a fulfilling life. They can, and ideally do, take place as we listen. Through these conversations, we are in dialogue with our spiritual source, with nature, with each other, and with our true self.

At this threshold at the center of our metaphorical labyrinth and all our thresholds, we can go deeper into this conversation of what no longer is true for us and what wants to become true.

TRY THIS: BEING AT THE THRESHOLD

There are many circles in life . . . Remember, do not get caught on just one circle; if you do, you will forever be going around in circles. Grasp the knowledge of that circle and then move on to the next. One day you will look up, and you will be at the center, and the mystery of life will be revealed to you.

—WA'NA'NEE'CHE' (Dennis Renault),
Native American Spirituality

This simple practice is both a way to meet up and cross a threshold in your life as much as it is a mind-training practice. It's a great practice when you feel stuck, resistant, or fearful of change. Perhaps you don't know how to turn around and head "out" from this place. This practice can be used at any threshold in our lives where we cross over from one place into another.

Choose a time period for this threshold; for example, a month, until the next full moon, or up to the day of a move. No need to design where you are going—simply acknowledge your threshold. You may know where you intend to arrive externally, so here you

> **Be *here*
> among *the living*, she said.**
>
> **And as I crossed the hills
> in daylight after, it was easy to remember a way.**
>
> **But at the dimming of days,
> familiar landmarks disappear.
> Then where, I wonder, do I head?—
> and where exactly is *here*?**
>
> **There is some hard turn to make, to make for
> the living ahead, that promises
> perhaps pain before blessing, and knowing
> I must cross myself first
> to get there.**

acknowledge your desire to move forward. Hold this conversation with this threshold. Allow for any discomfort and uncertainty.

Now begin to build your liminal threshold. This is how this practice is also a great mind-training practice. We can meet some aspect of the Great Unknown at all our thresholds, through conversation with all that arises. What are you going to leave while at the threshold? What are you willing and ready to let go of, to let die? What are you clearly no longer in agreement with?—your mother's version of you, for example.

This is a time pregnant with power. When you begin to build your liminal threshold, you can consider all that you are ready to let go of and place it at this inner threshold. During this time of being at your threshold, you can at any time leave beliefs, assumptions, relationships, agreements, fears, etc. Of course, here is the place we leave an aspect of our shadow, another expression of our dynamic.

You can also leave behind clutter, anything that will not serve you as you cross the threshold. So cleaning out a closet, ending a relationship, clearing a space for your creative work, even cleaning a garden of last season's debris—you are building your threshold with all that you are leaving behind.

I have worked with people who are suicidal and others who obsess about death. Some have come to me with repeated dreams of death. They want help. And I rely on the wisdom borrowed from Carl Jung when I ask them, "What in you needs to die?" Their soul is calling out for a death. Not an end to life, but an end to whatever prevents them from living fully and moving on across this threshold. They need to leave some outdated inner narratives, beliefs, fears, or resistance at their liminal threshold. So what wants to die? Notice I don't ask what are you willing to let die but what wants to die. First ask yourself: "What wants to die?" and then check in with your willingness and commitment to do whatever it takes to cross the threshold when it comes time. What agreements need to die? What relationship is dead? What are you giving your life force to that is no longer life-giving in return? If your job is killing you, why not kill your job? Leave it at the threshold. Is your addiction to alcohol ruining your life and your relationships? Let it die. What are you going to leave at the threshold as you stay present for this time of preparation for a transition? I once left my television at the threshold. Another time I left my attachment to recognition. (Right now, as I am housebound during the COVID-19 pandemic, I am at a threshold until the next full moon. I leave eating after 7 p.m., my worries about my daughter's future, my fears about money, my cluttered basement, clothes I no longer wear, and postponement of fun (like kayaking). I also leave behind the resistance to traveling alone to some foreign country.)

- A client shares her experience: "For me, my time at the threshold gave me something I had needed my entire life—the ability to say no, to let go, and leave behind someone or something as I moved on. It never occurred to me that I could dump dead weight, end lifeless relationships, and release the stuff of the past. And when I say stuff, I mean boxes of stuff. Once I got started, my first threshold was stockpiled with things, both material and psychological. And when I stepped through . . . I felt newly born."

At this point, you may feel distrustful of the new paradigm that is not fully known. How can we let go of something familiar when we are not certain what lies ahead? At one of my thresholds,

I let go of a beautiful life, leaving myself open to what was next. I must admit that I did hesitate at the threshold. We are not always just letting go of old, useless "stuff"; sometimes it is just time to move on.

What makes it initiatory and transformative is your courage to cross the threshold into something new and not fully known. There are sure to be surprises along the way! The threshold takes on the symbolic image of the snake shedding its skin again and again. And in this shedding, we create a new world for ourselves and for others.

To fully live and move forward with our life, we will have to step over many thresholds. These thresholds, once felt and realized, can be inspirational places of purpose and transformation of our choosing. There is no excuse for remaining stuck, staying behind, since all of life offers up these places of passage. Any fear and tension you feel emanates from the rules, agreements, and belief systems of the old paradigms that are attempting to hold on. Your inherent potentialities, what you are moving toward, rise up in your defense in different ways: in your dreams, body signals, synchronicities, physical symptoms, and sometimes illness. The liminal (nonphysical) threshold within the consciousness is the place of one's old identity and the edge of the new paradigm.

Simple rituals are potent points of transformation and mind training. Research has shown that acting out our intentions in such a way, calling on help from our Higher Power and the natural elements embodies these practices and their accompanying awareness. As I keep letting go of my fear of traveling alone at my threshold, I am getting ready to cross over the threshold into a time and place when I will travel abroad again.

Your Corporeal Threshold

The threshold is seen as a portal from one side of your life into the other side. You have already chosen a day when you will cross your threshold. You have been building up the energy of all you are going to leave behind.

Create a physical threshold somewhere outside, if possible; it can be made of cornmeal, stones, a line in the snow or sand, twigs sticking up out of the snow, or whatever creates a physical identity for your threshold. Your threshold can face east so when you move through it you are heading east, the direction of initiation, possibilities, the sunrise, and new beginnings. (But no rules.)

My recommendation is that you build your threshold a week or two before you walk through it, to let it build up some energy. You may place some physical objects there that you are letting go of, or you may visit this physical threshold from time to time to place psychological items there such as your fears or your dynamic. When you build your physical threshold, hold in your heart-mind an intention that represents the new paradigm: what you are moving toward or what you hope you are moving toward.

When you are ready to cross your threshold, approach the threshold with everything you are prepared to release. Hold your new intention in mind, the one you want to manifest in the world. Say out loud or in your mind everything you are leaving behind as you move across. Give it as much time as you like, while at the same time keeping it simple.

You can say these words out loud: "I no longer agree to . . . (for example) be afraid, hold myself back, give up, collect Beanie Babies, watch television, drink alcohol." Then continue to move toward or through your threshold. Leave behind all that is dead or all that represents the remainder of your dynamic. You may leave actual items at the threshold as well; I suggest they be organic and left to dissolve and perish. Say a prayer or sing a chant. Call for help from your Higher Power or the elements. Listen to your intuition and do what comes naturally.

Then step through the threshold. Know that you are entering a new paradigm, a new way of being. You are stepping into the Great Unknown of your beautiful, evolving life. You may keep your threshold in place and use it for future rituals or let it disintegrate and make a new one in the future.

Once over the threshold, you may find that a fear or some idea that you left at the threshold rises up. A simple practice is to say to that arrival: "I left you at the threshold." So when I board the plane to travel to Bhutan alone, and fear or anxiety rise up in me, I will repeat, "I left you at the threshold" and board the plane.

HOW NOT TO BE DISCOURAGED: CONVERSATIONS AS THRESHOLDS

As we face outward and focus on our efforts in the world, we will meet up with difficulty brought on by others. There may be circumstances in our lives that discourage us right down to the marrow. I doubt any of us gets through life free of discouragement. Like me, you may be discouraged by continual displays of bigotry and hatred. You may be in a job or relationship that undermines you. You may be like my friend and editor Anne Dillon who puts hours into saving our precious endangered elephants. Given how dire the situation appears to be for the elephants, how does she not get discouraged? Or you may have experienced a great loss or a considerable disappointment once or time and time again.

What does it mean to be discouraged? Something is dissing our courage: dis-courage-ment. When our courage is dissed, this may mean we withdraw when we would do better to engage, we close down when we would do better to open up, hold back when we would do better to take action. Discouragement can make us habitual and reactive rather than responsive and vulnerable. Discouraged, we may give in to the darkness around and inside of us.

BEATING DISCOURAGEMENT

The best and surest way to defeat discouragement is to keep the conversation going, to keep arriving at our thresholds, to return to the **Inner Labyrinth** and renew our exploration. Be part of the conversation, no matter what. A simple contemplative break that helps keep the conversation going could be to read some inspiring poetry or listen to a song. All poetry helps us move across those inner thresholds of discouragement or resistance.

The Climb

we climb the steep side of
this prairie hill strewed with sharp objects
and I know daughter, you will get cut
but don't stop

don't let the sharp objects
interrupt your flowering spirit
Because there is a there to get to
a greening so full of light
You will be willing to make
the climb again
and again.

—Julie Tallard Johnson

In Tibetan, *gyud* means "thread," "that which joins together." In this, its meaning is similar to that of the word *Tao*. Translated simply, *Tao* is the unifying principle within all life. You might say that everything that expresses the intrinsic nature of all phenomena is our *gyud*. When we take hold of the red thread, we connect everything to everything else. As we turn around, we pick up the red thread that we have placed down to get here, to then take us out in the world, into our next story, our next encounters, into a fearless state of belonging.

FACING OUTWARD: PICKING UP THE RED THREAD

As we become holders of the red thread, we also become an expression of something that can join all of us together. In the myth of the Minotaur, many individuals who came before Theseus didn't have hold of a red thread but successfully confronted the Minotaur. However, they never found their way back out of the labyrinth and died trapped inside.

Theseus means "to place down," as demonstrated by his actions wherein he placed the red thread down for himself and then for others. If we have done our inner work successfully, we, too, have placed the red thread upon our inner path and are able to gather the thread back up again and pass it on to others. In further development of the "receiving and giving" motif, our journey in is about receiving the teachings and realizations. We have received many realizations having gone to the center of our **Inner Labyrinth** again and again. Our walk out is about sharing our knowings with others. A reminder here that these thresholds and passages and returnings are constant, and each time we turn around and cross a threshold, we feel more deeply rooted in our true nature and our belonging to the world.

All of this inner work is so we can live actively, faithfully, and truthfully in the outer world in order to make a difference simply by the way we live our day-to-day lives.

MOVING OUTWARD

We never reach the end of our inner journey; every time we experience some personal realization, there is fostered from within us a myriad of new possibilities that can be parlayed into other concrete actions moving forward. Life now, walking onward, will continually evolve in personal and meaningful ways for each and every one of us.

Let's take this down to the purely physical level. When I walk, I commit to a certain destination, perhaps a broken tree that is about two miles from my home. This way, in my round trip, I am certain to have a four-mile walk. In a similar way, when we journey into our metaphorical labyrinth, we have given ourselves a place to go—inward to our center. Now, at this threshold, we turn around and start walking back out, gathering up our red thread as we go. We give ourselves a place to go—to our continued places of belonging and wholeness, and to community where we experience and co-create reality.

Beginning Begins

Thoughts to stop me
cold in my tracks,
pile around in heaps like worn-out rail ties.

My legs too, seem of a hard poisoned wood.
How to bend and walk toward the calling,
beyond the frozen here and now
into blazing who knows what? - to find the next,
the new,
to where beginning begins?

I might just stay on the still, frozen ground.
But *here's how*, without a word, say the Cranes.
Those pencil-legged champions
of faith,
show up again, lifting the burdensome question
of how,
in their *just go*
of migration.

They don't even lift their heads, but say
what's the question?
Just go where you're expected.
The ground will thaw under your steps.

CHAPTER SEVEN

GATHERING THE THREAD ON THE WAY OUT: GIVING SHAPE TO THE WORLD

> *Action, like a sacrament, is the visible form of an invisible spirit, an outward manifestation of an inward power. But as we act, we not only express what is in us and help give shape to the world; we also receive what is outside us, and we reshape our inner lives. When we act, the world acts back, and we and the world are co-created.*
>
> —Parker J. Palmer

GIVING SHAPE TO THE WORLD

The move out from the center symbolically represents our being in the "outer labyrinth," where we are actively in relationship with others, in community, and bring forth our gift of true self to others. In one of my conversations with Parker, he said, "A lot of things happen before things happen." We were talking about that magical element prior to and behind our actions and their "happenings." There is always something happening behind the scenes of our life that helps move our life forward. Continuing with the theme of being in conversation from the previous chapter, the active life is engaged in this conversation in a myriad of ways, passing through many thresholds.

As long as we remain engaged and in conversation with the world inside and around us, we move into the next years and decades as an active participant in them. In the myth, Theseus was guided by Ariadne to continually move forward.

In gathering the red thread on our way out, we open to our destiny in the world. We, too, must find our way out and into our lives, an inward and outward expedition that is repeated over and over, each time yielding new possibilities.

DESTINY VERSUS FATE

A great analogy for me in understanding the critical difference between fate and destiny is the path of a mountain stream. Over the years and decades the stream erodes a channel down the mountainside, typically to an ocean. Rainwater and the mountain's formation created the fated path of this stream. However, given how large the mountainside is, there are many other possible pathways for the stream. Knowing and making other pathways constitutes our ability to co-create our destinies with the mountain.

Each of us has a fate and a destiny. *Fate is how we reference the original path made for us—that which was beyond our control, starting from and including conception. We cannot change our fate, nor are we responsible for having caused it.* Fate must be acknowledged. For example, you may have been born into catastrophe like me, introduced to alcoholism, abuse, and neglect from birth. This is part of my fate. I had no control over who my parents were. But my innate gifts and who I was at birth are also my fate.

Those happenings in life over which we do have influence and are at least partially responsible for are aspects not of fate but of destiny. While we can't move mountains, we have the superpower to alter and transform what is possible for us, to change the path of our lives. *Destiny is what we do with our fate. Our individual and collective destiny must be actively discovered and fulfilled. Destiny can bring forth more of what fate has brought us, especially our gifts located in the aquifers of our inner self.*

Destiny is our journey to becoming who we truly are; it's evolutionary, having the capacity to move us forward. Destiny is co-creative. This dance with destiny impels us to listen to our inner knowing. Destiny involves making choices, and fulfilling it requires heroines. The red thread can guide us out the labyrinth to our destinies, as it helped Theseus to his. But we can too easily forget we have this thread, becoming lost or stuck or disoriented. We can take all that we were born with—the beautiful and catastrophic—to help make the world beautiful. We can realize our partnership with others and all of life by realizing the destiny inherent in our fates. How's that for a paradox!?

To help others co-create their destinies, we must first claim our own. Also, like Theseus, we are motivated by intentions to help others, to alleviate the suffering of others. We see ourselves as heroines, as leaders, and we act accordingly.

A favorite passage of mine, which points to the suffering that can occur when we don't work with our fate and open to our destinies is from Jesus:

> *If you bring forth what is within you*
> *what is within you will save you.*
> *If you do not bring forth that which is within you*
> *What you do not bring forth will destroy you.*
>
> —Elaine Pagels, *The Gnostic Gospels*

HEY, THERE'S A PEARL ATTACHED TO YOUR FOREHEAD!

> *Huang Po scolded us for being like someone who, without knowing it, has a pearl attached to his forehead, yet goes searching all around the world for that same pearl. Perhaps we'll even search outside the world into hells, heavens, and the Brahma worlds. Not seeing what is stuck to our foreheads, we seek all around the world, and if that's not enough, in the other realms. So please, just for awhile, look very closely to see what is there on your forehead and how you are going to get your hands on it.*
>
> —Buddhadasa Bhikkhu, *Heartwood of the Bodhi Tree*

So much energy can go into proving ourselves to others and even to ourselves. We can't be trying to prove ourselves and at the same time express the truth of our inherent gifts or share our gifts to help shape the world. It takes vulnerability and courage to bring forth our truest selves. As my daughter experienced during her first years of college, I witnessed her being enthused by some choices and activities and drained by others. I would say to her: "How does it feel to paint that mural?" and encourage her to notice those endeavors that brought her happiness and satisfaction without needing validation and approval from others.

> **I lie down to sleep,
> my head at the feet of the masters, gone now.
> Remember, to lay open
> mind and heart is all—and they,
> miners of precious Truth,
> they drop pearls, flash ruby and sapphire
> down through dreams, asking little enough in return:
> now you, pass it on.**

TAKE NOTICE OF THIS

None of us has to go anywhere special to discover that pearl. All we have to do is take notice. Notice how we feel when involved in various activities. Is this activity draining you or feeding you? How? What are your emotions when involved in this activity? Do you feel engaged or bored? Notice what brings energy and satisfaction. Notice what fills you up in the action itself and doesn't demand that you obtain external approval.

Is your life, most of the time, true to these gifts and inner callings? Are you motivated from within to simply express yourself, or are you motivated from without to prove yourself somehow?

What you love is your pearl, and it is right there. We all must discover that pearl on our forehead, know what we love, and express it. Many of us may have to wash floors or drive school buses to generate money to help us fulfill our callings. As long as these jobs and environments are safe for the soul, you will have the energy to perform your day job as well as pursue your callings. I have noticed that when my daughter does a project that appears to be a setup for her to "prove herself"—sadly we find this in our places of education and vocation—her energy is drained and her work not as satisfying to her. And this "forced" work typically isn't her best. In like manner, notice where you, too, are pushed and feel forced to produce something.

That said, of course there is a great discipline involved in giving shape to the world. *Expressive action is the way we make a contribution to the larger scheme of things because it brings our unique qualities into play. And all our expressive actions are fed from within; they are consciously chosen and pursued. This is what Parker means when he refers to contemplative action— action that is rooted in consciousness and purposefulness.*

You will discover that you naturally have the energy and discipline to pursue what you love.

> Too many paths of others in you,
> she said. Lots,
> it's true, straight on through me.
> I am the road well traveled it turns out,
> and don't think there's any other way
> to traverse this life. We walk on through others
> and they through us.
> The hard stomps, tip-toes, and dance-floor moves
> all evident in this mud.
> Can you see your own soul marks? Look closely,
> oh yes they're here.

THE DANCING WARRIOR: CONTEMPLATIVE ACTION

Because of our continued willingness and vulnerability to go into ourselves and face our indifferences and other internal shadow selves, we can trust our choices and actions. The active life, versus the reactive or habitual life, is aided by such contemplation. Since we have explored our inner world through contemplation, with a commitment to continue to do so, our actions are contemplative at their root. Therefore such actions will be of benefit, no matter how small we may deem them to be. Such actions are linked to our collective destinies; they are connected to who we truly are.

When my daughter struggles with her choices, particularly involving her creative life, I encourage her to focus on being authentic over being original. To have her focus on trying to be original and unique encourages her to be competitive rather than cooperative and engaged. This pressure to be original discourages a cooperative exploration of how her action may involve others and how her actions may be useful. In our authentic undertakings we sense our usefulness. This authenticity is, too, a courageous vulnerability.

> *Piglet was so excited at the idea of being Useful that he forgot to be frightened any more.*
>
> —A. A. Milne, *Winnie-the-Pooh*

Just being ourselves can be courageous and vulnerable enough in a world that often wants to dictate to us how and who we should be.

TRY THIS: AN INFORMED DANCE: REFRAMING

We can reframe our experiences to give ourselves relevant and timely possibilities when our opportunities seem limited. Then, through such contemplative action, we allow for an even larger scope of possibilities to emerge.

This particular contemplative activity is an invitation to reframe an experience you are going into that is challenging. Are you feeling stuck, held back, regretful, or hindered in some way? Are you in an unfavorable circumstance that you can't escape? Are you at a difficult threshold?

There are many times in our life when we can't, and maybe shouldn't, get out of our circumstances. We have chosen to stay put but still feel trapped and immobilized. We may be holding ourselves or another captive in a mindset we can't seem to shake. Or we are on a continue loop of negativity about our life circumstances. All of these scenarios present optimal opportunities to reframe our experience.

THE SACRAMENT OF REFRAMING

We always frame our experiences with assumptions, beliefs, historical narratives, agreements, and expectations. Each experience is framed with storylines. In a reframe, we re-story our experience and give it a new narrative.

I looked back at my notes and reflected on the reframe that was involved with my turning sixty, my daughter leaving for college, and my husband retiring. The story that framed the experience of my only daughter leaving for college and my turning sixty had been: *I have a lot to regret; I can't do it over. I have lost my spiritual community and won't find another. Life's best is over. I won't do well with Lydia gone (I doubt my capacity).*

I have a lot to regret; I can't do it over.

I won't do well with Lydia gone (I doubt my capacity). | **MY DAUGHTER LEAVING FOR COLLEGE AND MY TURNING SIXTY** | **I have lost my spiritual community and won't find another.**

Life's best is over.

Here's what I recommend: create a box—a frame—and in the center identify a difficult experience. Identify a threshold or confusing or hard situation you are in at the time. Then on the outside of each side, identify a belief, an assumption, or a perception. In the middle of the frame, name the story. For me it was: Turning Sixty and Daughter Leaving for College. In doing this exercise, you end up with the experience you are framing in the middle, and the beliefs and assumptions and perceptions on the outside.

Sometimes our story, our way of framing things, is simply outdated. But more often than not, if we are struggling, it is because we are framing things in a negative and often hostile way. The process of trying to reframe something for ourselves is where most of the mojo comes from. As we even play around with how we might frame this experience in a new way, new pathways are being made in our brains and in our lives. Pat, a woman in one of my red thread circles, reframed her experience after she received a little money from a deceased ex-husband. This money came to her unexpectedly and she initially framed it by saying "I don't deserve it, I didn't earn it, I feel compelled to give it away before I even truly receive it, and I am afraid to take it." Then she created a second box/frame with the same circumstance in the middle: My deceased ex left me money. Then, this being the reframe, she took the time to identify life-enhancing beliefs and responses. Her reframe: "I deserve this and have the ability to receive this. I am grateful for this surprise. And I have earned it as he owed me more than this due to his borrowing money from me. I am free to give it away if I want."

Here is the *reframe* of my example: *I have great memories with my daughter. I am in my second adulthood. I am open to more that is possible now with Lydia gone. I can and will create a new spiritual community.*

I have great memories with my daughter.

I can and will create a new spiritual community.

MY DAUGHTER LEAVING FOR COLLEGE AND MY TURNING SIXTY

I am in my second adulthood.

I am open to more that is possible now with Lydia gone.

Once we have reframed our situation we step into and live our new and evolving story. We take this reframe and act on it. I came to trust my capacity to navigate this new chapter in my life. And in the reframing of this inevitable separation and change I discovered I was entering my second adulthood. This reframe became my new and evolving story: As I move into and through my sixties I am now in my second adulthood. This made for so much possibility. I can at this late date be excited for new things, or old things made new.

One question you can ask yourself is, *What no longer serves you in the story?* I asked myself: *Does my regret serve me or my daughter?* The answer was: Not in the least. As I shared in an earlier chapter, such emotions as regret can spill over, and in this example my daughter could be burdened by my regret. And, along with my reframe I hosted the edge of my regrets.

To further explore your reframe:

- Contemplate what no longer serves you in the old framing of your experience.
- You could place everything surrounding the old reframe on a threshold.
- Identify what part of the story is still trying to frame your present experience.
- Determine some of the culturally endorsed views that may frame your experience. For instance, how does our culture typically respond to aging or separation and individuation? You can host the edges here.

TRY THIS: INSTANT REFRAME

Reframing is a reliable technique to improve any experience. When we actively reframe, things look different to us so we experience things differently. Have you ever framed something with an "I'm screwed"? A quick reframe to this could be: "Oh, this is tough but possible." Again, how we frame a situation—even a future situation—will greatly determine our experience. After you have used this technique a few times, notice when you are in a negative frame of mind. This can be around something fairly benign, such as being bothered by how your partner loads the dishwasher. Then, "on the spot," reframe your experience.

Notice what thoughts and assumptions are making this a negative experience, then reframe it . . . but be realistic. Keep it simple.

You can't simply reframe an abusive marriage, the fact that a tree fell on your house, or that your parents were neglectful and alcoholic. We can't reframe fate. We can reframe our experiences and responses so that we empower ourselves to get out of a bad marriage, see the blessing in a fallen tree, and harvest what we can from our broken childhood. We can co-create our destinies.

REFRAME THROUGH RECLAIMING STOLEN WORDS

Anything we do to reframe our internal pictures of the world reframes our outer world and experiences. My initial introduction to Parker was when I heard him speak on public radio over two decades ago. (I suppose this ages us both quite a bit!) In his discussion, he talked about "stolen words" and how we need to claim back certain words and terms like patriotic and democratic. We have to claim and reframe them by using them.

Words and phrases, especially ones shared in our collective psyche, are powerful brokers. We find ourselves believing without reservation that north is up and south is down. We find ourselves being scared of someone because they are a Christian or a Muslim. Or, war is patriotic but peace is unpatriotic. Words like Muslim and immigrant are being stolen and framed for political purposes.

We reclaim them by using them in our contemplations and in our conversations. As a classic example, the word peace, for me, is patriotic. When I express this in words and actions, I am claiming back the term patriotic. In our actions and in our speech, we must use and speak out forbidden and stolen words, reframing them when necessary. "I am a monger of peace."

Listen to what you are agreeing to when someone tells you something. "I did it out of love." "This is what a patriot does." "Immigrants are not true Americans." "Everyone wants to be an American."

Consider every word we carry as being sacred and itself a container of a potent elixir or poison. You not only carry this word around with you, affecting your psychophysical body, but when spoken you impact the world around you. You release the elixir or poison from the bottle. When a word is stolen and we haven't claimed it back, the vibration and meaning of the stolen word is the one carried in our psyches as well as the one heard and felt by others. One way to claim a stolen word is to use it in ways that others resist. This would include those words that some group has taken possession of, and yet you want to lay some claim to as well, such as patriotic or immigrants. For example, are we not a nation of immigrants? Do seeing immigrants as the stranger protect us in any way? Do immigrants generate unemployment? Are we just one big melting pot?

Presently it is challenging to claim such titles as healer, counselor, leader, social worker, or teacher when these roles have frequently come to be associated with such negative connotations. So, through our conscious actions and expression of these words and roles, we reframe the world; we help restore the world to its truer state of being. Also, such words as leader, teacher, healer, and heroine have been reserved for the special few, when in fact each of us who has hold of the red thread has the capacity to hand it to others, to teach and to lead (more on this in Chapter 9).

A FEW OTHER WAYS TO REFRAME

Spiritual teachings poetry, stories are ways to reframe our perspectives and experiences. Each time we open up and consider such messages we reframe our view and therefore our experience, even if slightly.

Here are some other reframing options:

- Use a poem or song or myth to contemplate and reframe a situation.
- Read from another author or teacher's perspective instead of the one you are typically drawn to.
- Go for a walk holding a question in mind.
- Participate in a circle of trust, an Al-Anon meeting, or other circles where skillful dialogue and questions are practiced.

Anytime we are willing to take a risk, step out of what we may routinely or habitually say or do, and act, we are risking our comfort, we are being vulnerable and courageous." Taking action is a vulnerability of its own and when rooted in our truth, is a risk that will result in something real.

 From where? no place, except the mind of god—which
does not make you a figment. Your name
you can recall another time. Just for now, try not to mind
all your bumping about. It's that way
we learn to see
in the dark. And you must not think you're alone.

WHEN THE SOUL CALLS, LISTEN.

Listening to what calls us means to listen to what our highest and wildest self wants for us. This may take the form of messages encrypted in your dreams, encounters with another, or some feverish call within that can't be shaken or discounted by usual measures of denial. These encounters are like a sound through the dense forest that starts out quiet and increases, as they get closer. Or they may be more like a forest fire that rages and gets hotter as it nears your home. You will have to evacuate or be destroyed. You will have to venture out from all that you think you know and have if you want to find out what is calling you.

Listening to our inner callings—which some may call soul—is not just about moving toward something external. Or when it includes some external changes, it should not be all about that. Often we leave a marriage or a job only to move toward another person or a new job. If this is the case, our energy should not be distracted by that new person or that new job. For when our focus is too much on another person or situation, we will likely miss the actual journey itself, which is where the gifts of soul are offered and is what the soul's calling is all about.

Hearing soul burn through the forest in our direction is the call of the Creative, of the Wild Woman or Man. It's is the sound of the Great Mother-Father-God reaching out to us. The soul arrives to open the door, to create a passageway for you to open up to the fullness of your life. This has nothing to do with religion. This is a listening to our selves from deep within—a time of encountering and knowing who we are and what we truly want.

Acting from our more soulful origins depends a great deal on emotional awareness and trusting one's intuition and one's personal experiences. Emotional awareness is key, for if our journey is held only in the intellect of the mind with fine words we will miss both the message of our soul and the journey itself.

As you act from your truest callings continue to clear away the negative chatter that may exist in your mind and in your environment. Negative chatter in your mind may take the form of self-talk wherein you say "I should," "I have to," or "I can't." Oh, I love this one: "Who do I think I am?" The negative chatter in your environment may be due to the drama of others, or dogma that you break out of and are reprimanded for, others' stories of your experience, and/or others' demands or influence.

We can't know what's going to happen as we continue to listen and act upon our inner callings. This is why we may have a tendency to latch on to something or someone when fear and anxiety arise. When we feel the fire of soul we may panic. Our fear then ties our ride to the wave of change with an attachment to something or someone because we can't control how or where things will play out and we are comforted by the presence of an objective to aim for or another person to place our future on.

Don't do it. Don't latch on to something that only appears to guarantee safety and security.

Many people seek my guidance after they have arrived in a new destination or relationship and are confused by the way it is limiting them and the unhappiness it has brought them. At this point they, as you are now, moving out and into the world. They rushed or forced a certain outcome and lost an opportunity to open up to all that was truly possible. But as we have all heard, it is the journey not the destination that rewards us the most. As evidenced by these unhappy people, in trying to control the journey, in a attempt to control the outcome, we may miss so much!

Also, others may want to interfere or influence our journey's outcome. This most likely means that they may not be on their own journey or/and are overly focused on or invested in ours. As John O'Donohue expresses in *Anam Cara*, "You can never love another person unless you are equally involved in the beautiful, but difficult spiritual work of learning to love yourself." Don't be distracted by another's intellect or solutions, or a religion's guarantees, even when it is offered up in beautiful words and slogans. Instead, see that everything in front of you is speaking to you—rely on what each moment brings and, as best you can, remain curious and open to communication with your inner callings and your spiritual source (whatever that may be for you).

Your truest self, the you from birth wants to bring you to a tipping point where you will continue to say "yes" to your destiny; where you will act on your inner callings.

WHAT HAPPENS WHEN WE DON'T LISTEN TO SOUL'S CALLING?

When you sense that rumbling of change in your heart and belly, or beneath your feet, soul is calling you and trying to get your attention. Soul is calling you when you feel the heat of the fire or hear some sound approaching through the woods but cannot yet see it. If we don't listen to soul, initially, we tend to have an emotional crisis, then a spiritual one, and then, a physical crisis that brings us to our knees (literally).

An emotional crisis can take the form of anxiety, grief, depression, fear (especially of loss), anger, and any emotion that feels disruptive and overwhelming.

A spiritual crisis brings out such questions as *Who am I? Where and to whom do I belong? Why has God abandoned me? What do I believe? What can I trust? Why is this happening to me?* Spiritual principles and beliefs you have relied on in the past may become points of pain and confusion.

A physical crisis can start out with breathlessness and various aches and pains that trigger fear and anxiety. These aches and pains start to get our attention; it's all about getting our attention. How many people have shared that some physical crisis brought them back into a truer path for their life? How many have spoken about the injury they got that, for them, was their final wake-up call to follow their heart and soul to a truer (or next) calling?

Ideally, we want to listen to the emotional calling from within us so we don't have to experience a spiritual or physical crisis. Fortunately, an emotional or spiritual crisis is hard to ignore. A physical is impossible to ignore—but many still do.

I borrow from a prayer offering in John O'Donohue's *Anam Cara* to help me recognize my soul's calling: *I pray for the grace of recognition; I pray for the recognition to know when to act and when not to; I pray to know what to listen to and what to leave behind; I pray for the grace to recognize true friendship; I pray for the grace of recognition of my true belonging; I pray for the grace of recognition when it comes to others and how I can serve them as I listen to my soul.*

Finally, such a journey is not selfish but helps bring to fruition the soulfulness of every living thing. The implication is clear. Because we are all a part of the whole, when we heal something in ourselves, we heal it in the world. When we act from our truest calling, our actions transform the world around us. Each individual consciousness is connected to all other forms of consciousness; therefore, personal healing encourages collective healing.

THE TAKE AWAY

At the end of an evening's circle, I like everyone to consider their "takeaway." What are we taking away from that evening's sharing of contemplations, questions, explorations, and stories? A takeaway ideally leads to action or is an action. Often a takeaway is to further contemplate some topic that was discussed or personal realization that was shared. Even so, keeping these to ourselves would be like remaining at the center of the labyrinth. After all this internal work, we must gather our knowings and share them with others through our vulnerability and action.

While writing this chapter I felt a division in my life. I noticed how my writing life encouraged me to remain in the center of my labyrinth—just me and my ideas. I was spending too much time writing and not enough time with others through engagement in community and in relationship. So I scheduled some time with family, friends, and community over the next month. That was my takeaway.

The day I made this insight I decided to meet up with a friend that night to attend a reading at a lovely local bookstore—Arcadia, in Spring Green, Wisconsin. The featured author was John McKnight, coauthor of *The Abundant Community*.

We could say that connection is the antidote to consumption. It begins with identifying the neighborhood treasures waiting to be given.

—John McKnight and Peter Block,
The Abundant Community

So, Dear Reader, what is your takeaway?

> Leaves, seeming of a collective mind, hurried past me.
> Each of us, in our own way,
> was stirred by that force,
> sometimes called the Wind.
> But I wasn't fated to be blown—rigid, same as they.
> Wind, now I know, can be ridden
> many ways.

CHAPTER EIGHT

RETURNING TO THE WORLD: THE THREAD OF TRUE COMMUNITY

Whether we know it or not, like it or not, honor it or not, we are embedded in community. Whether we think of ourselves as biological creatures or spiritual beings or both, the truth remains: we were created in and for a complex ecology of relatedness, and without it we wither and die. This simple fact has critical implications: community is not a goal to be achieved but a gift to be received.

—Parker J. Palmer

The idea and love of place has guided much of my life.
—John McKnight, *The Abundant Community*

THE MORE THE MERRIER

On one of my visits with Parker, I introduced him to Rebecca Cecchini, the poet whose contributions season this book. Shouldn't every project and community have a resident poet? I think so. Poets have been part of that thread throughout my life that not only binds but brings together. Poetry for me brings differences together, turns contradiction into a paradoxical narrative that reaches our hearts and souls. Poetry makes it possible for me to step into another's world and more deeply step from my own.

Parker appreciates poetry as a way of bringing soul into our gatherings, helping us examine our lives so we may live them from the inside out: "Inner truth is best conveyed by the language of the heart, of image and metaphor, of poetry, and it is best understood by people for whom poetry is a second language." Poetry doesn't insist but invites, just as a true community does. Community can be an invitation to discover and express our gifts of who we are and what we have to offer one another.

During my conversation with Parker on this visit, I read him several of Rebecca's poems as a way of introducing her. I mentioned that she would be contributing verses to help the reader of my book take contemplative breaks. His response: "The more the merrier"—a simple, profound truth. Every worthy project is an invitation to join in with others, invite others into the conversations, and bring our shared gifts out into the open, into community. Just so, this chapter borrows from John McKnight's teachings and his book *The Abundant Community*. It also borrows from many other sources and people who have contributed to creating true communities. The more the merrier.

A GENEROSITY OF HOSPITALITY

For me, the message of this book and the myth of Theseus' journey is: *We are each here to take the inner and outer journey in service of the true self and true community.*

Again we come back to the power of receiving first and then giving—community needs to be understood as "a gift to be received." And as we receive this gift of community we are gifting, too, through our receptivity (see discussion of the Three R's on page 63). But when we cannot receive community first, we are left with nothing to give. In my Buddhist practices, this is about generosity of spirit.

Friends comment on how generous I am. And I want this to be true, always. But it is a quality that I often have to work to cultivate because it does not always arise spontaneously. I have found myself jealous and competitive at times. When jealousy came knocking, it emerged from a false perception that there are a limited amount of goodies to go around. It is as if there is a limit to the love, friendship, appreciation, talent, and all the abundance that living in true community has to offer each of us. There is much in our culture that encourages this fear of lack, and so we are also encouraged to approach others with suspicion, gearing us up to compete for benefits. We see this when the ridiculously rich are not satisfied with their millions and continue to dominate and hoard more money, more stuff, more whatever. They, and sometimes we, have lost touch with the true abundance of community and our belonging. This goes back to the empty self syndrome where we feel there is never enough and we are never satisfied, at least for long.

When we feel jealous it's like going to the market with a closed fist, with our hands in our pockets. There is so much abundance to receive but we can't be open to it when we're jealous or closed down in some way. Every time I choose generosity, my generosity and joy are made more abundant. Then this generosity allows me to receive and, in my abundance, I am able to give again. And again.

Generosity is one of the "six perfections" in Buddhist practice. These perfections are qualities and states of being that can result in a more awakened heart. The six perfections are: generosity, ethical discipline, enthusiastic effort, patience, concentration, and wisdom. Generosity is the first *paramita* (invaluable quality) of these six. All others are dependent upon the understanding and expression of this one. All are understood as qualities that unfold and manifest from within our minds. These perfections are another red thread given to us by spiritual teachers of the past. And, as with generosity, as we perfect (receive) each of these qualities in our lives, more joy and abundance are experienced. This way we have these qualities to give to others. The idea is to discover and cultivate these red thread qualities so they may ripen in us. All of the other perfections are dependent upon a heart of generosity—the act of correct receiving and giving.

Such individual traits are also communal traits. Our gifts, our relationships, our stories, our hospitality, our enthusiastic effort, our disciplines, our patience, and our silence are all properties of an abundant, true community. Parker encourages a quality of hospitality, which for me is the quintessential expression of generosity. Hospitality invites a friendship with the world. All things that are hospitable to our soul are hospitable to others.

We are better able to explore and learn, and to make conscious choices in hospitable spaces. We must explore our abilities and willingness for connectedness. On arrival in any place where there are others, the first gift to receive is hospitality. The first gift to give is hospitality. Sadly though, we are hard-wired toward separation and division.

WIRED TOWARD SEPARATION

If a man settles in a certain place and does not bring forth the fruit of that place, the place itself casts him out.
—The Desert Monks, taken from *Apophthegmata Patrum: The Sayings of the Desert Fathers*

What feels true for me is that we feel like an outcast when we do not bring forth the fruit of a place because we do not know how to receive the gifts of community. Or, we are in a false community where the fruit is synthetic and unable to nurture the true self. We want to be connected to others but often don't know how. We understand, from deep within, that being in authentic relationship is necessary for us to feel our aliveness.

In my upbringing, community was "out there," something foreign, where the "other" spoke a language I didn't understand. My siblings and I were discouraged from joining in, and we didn't belong to any associations such as churches, clubs, or neighborhood groups. My family had a way of making the stranger strange and unapproachable; they were not inclusive of others who were perceived to be different from themselves. The other, the outsider, and the larger institutions to which we had no access or control were always seen to be the cause of any number of the family's problems.

When my parents socialized, they hosted cocktail hours and football parties, to which my parents would invite my father's customers. I witnessed card nights with neighbors and many other parties where alcohol seemed to be the most revered guest. As I got older, my siblings and mother ridiculed me for not lightening up and joining the party.

I did try to join in at times, but groups such as Brownies and the Girl Scouts were extremely uncomfortable for me, for I felt like an intruder who didn't know their ways. And I didn't know the language or ways of community or communal relationship. Any attempts to join in resulted in me feeling more isolated. Even in my young teen years when I was sent to a week-long camp, I ended up getting in trouble because I couldn't seem to go along with team activities. I either resisted being told what to do or I did my own thing. A camp counselor pulled me aside and said that I was not ever going to fit in. Then, in a further coincidence, she was my high school running coach the following fall. She made it clear to me and the other teachers that I was a misfit. A delinquent. Sadly, these labels felt accurate, even to me.

I did discover a sense of community when I was accepted into our country's first alternative "free" school: Malcolm Shabazz High School in Madison, Wisconsin (named after Malcolm X). I attended my last two years of high school there. Its teachers were hospitable, open, and flexible. If not for this hospitable experience, I would not have chosen to go on to college and pursue my vocation as a social worker. I would not likely be here writing these words for you.

In reality, there were places of community at camp and at Girl Scouts, but again I didn't know how to identify or receive community. Therefore, I was ill equipped to give myself to the community. I started my volunteering at the age of thirteen. On my block was a daycare facility for children with special needs. One summer day, I introduced myself to them and asked if I might volunteer there. They happily said yes, and a few times a week I played and interacted with the children there. At the end of the summer the facility gave me a volunteer award.

I took it but I couldn't receive it. After tucking it away for a few weeks, I burned it. Somehow I had come to believe I didn't deserve this acknowledgment. I was wholly lacking in the ability to receive the gift of community in this way. I didn't even have a "community of family," because we were kept divided, even from within the family.

I didn't realize it at the time, and not fully until recently, that my search for spiritual connection was just as much—if not more—about connecting with other people as it was about connecting with a spiritual source. My search for God and community began at age eight when I would walk to the local church to visit with the Lutheran minister and attend church on my own.

My spiritual searching when I was younger, and my continued

spiritual explorations today, had at their core the desire to belong, to be part of a true community. I believe this is accurate for all of us. Most people I counsel are in search of love, belonging, and an authentic sense of place. Many don't know what love and belonging look like.

My studying and consciously exploring community kicked in when I ventured off to college. This interest and passion developed during my graduate years.

How true for so many of us: our truest self knows what we need, so although we may undergo a fair amount of trial and error on our path of "arriving," arrive we shall! My master's thesis was on the formation of support groups. I decided to research the help that was out there for families of the mentally ill when a college professor of mine happened to say: "There are some groups that simply cannot organize, such as the mentally ill." An outcome of my research was my first book, *Hidden Victims, Hidden Healers: An Eight-Stage Healing Process for Families and Friends of the Mentally Ill*. In the early to mid '90s I traveled throughout the United States and Canada, and then to Australia, to form eight-stage groups for families as well as to train facilitators.

Yet a more personal experience of community continued to elude me. As citizens and leaders we must be careful not to depend on or hide behind the roles we hold, such as counselor or facilitator. I did help form communities but often put my own need for community aside to do my work.

Of course, this co-creating of self and community will be an ongoing journey for me, and for you. As a counselor and facilitator of circles I have to be particularly mindful to find places where I can receive community as well as give it.

Parker's greatest gift to me, which I continue to receive and share, is wisdom about how to best co-create and be part of true community in all of my relationships and assemblies. In my various circles that I hold for others, I borrow significantly from his Circles of Trust model.

At that more recent, dark passage that I have written about in the previous chapter, having to do with my spiritual sangha, the disappointment I felt came down to a lack of community. The gatherings of the sangha were all about following the spiritual teachings in a certain way, and community wasn't encouraged. Instead, in this setting, community was a distant cousin. Although often we would share in ritual or conversation, always, at the core of any interaction or practice, was the dogma. It was all about the teachings—understanding and practicing them in the right way—and performing the rituals properly if you wanted to benefit from your efforts. In all of this, we had to approach our gatherings in a way that excluded any personal discernment and vulnerability with one another. When I shared this story with Parker he said, "unfortunately, community in our culture too often means a group of people who go crashing through the woods together, scaring away the very thing we seek."

Although the teachings within this sangha were great resources of contemplation and exploration, there were no spiritual friends to dialogue with, to explore the many issues that such spiritual teachings can bring up. We were on our own in a way that discouraged revealing our more personal natures and questions. And, as I have shared in a previous chapter, I was constantly being "corrected" in my actions. Sadly, a lot of these corrections came when I had braved myself to join in and be part of a ritual or festivities. Here I was able and willing to receive community, but it was not offered.

My final visit to the sangha came when one of the nuns asked if I wanted to play a role in an upcoming ceremony. She went out of her way to email me about it. She said that I would recite a chant with two other nuns to honor His Holiness the Dalai Lama. I appreciated this invitation because I had never been contacted outside of our gatherings. I had never been invited to participate; in the past I had always stepped up and volunteered. So, after having not been an active member of the sangha for some time, I decided that yes, I would join in and participate in this ceremony. I was skeptically optimistic that maybe this was a role I could fill; a place I could belong.

Having been sent the brief chant I would recite, I then showed up for the occasion. The nun who had invited me was approached by another nun and, within earshot of me, was told that I was not to take part in the ceremony after all; there was someone more suited to perform the chant. Hearing this, I thought, *Okay, just be with this . . . just go with it.* (I value just being present in various situations to see what emerges.)

The ceremony unfolded without incident. At the end of it, I was asked to help pass out the food that would be served. Based on prior experience, I knew that it would first be served to the monks. So I approached them, placing their bags of food on the small meditation tables in front of them. When I came to the nun who said I should not participate in the ritual, I placed my offerings on the small table in front of her, where there also happened to be some books.

"You are not to do that," she said. I almost laughed and cried out loud. Now what?! I thought.

"The food is not to be placed on top of prayer books."

I looked down and saw that some of the bag that contained the food was on the corner of one of her books. I adjusted this and moved on.

After leaving that day I have not gone back. I am sad about the teachings I may be missing. As regards my family of origin, I am also sad about the family connections I will never experience with them. However, now I am able to partake in both spiritual teachings and community from Santikaro and elsewhere in my day to day life. I am also a member of various clubs and associations where alcohol consumption doesn't dominate and dogma is not essential.

As well, I have taken hold of Parker's teachings. These took the form of that invisible but strong red thread that held me together with the hidden knowing that there are places where I will feel my belonging, places where my foibles and limits are as welcome as my gifts. These communities feed my soul and allow me to feel abundance. As revealed in my stories here, the red thread of Parker's teachings help me to keep hold of my Buddhist heritage as well as remain in conversation with my spiritual source. Such a paradoxical bonus!

That sangha, and sadly my family, were, at the end of the day, false communities where my true self was forced into hiding in order to simply survive. But the silver lining in this cloud was that this lack drove me to find my true self in true community. I now go where there is real hospitality, where differences are celebrated rather than scorned. This sense of true community is an invitation that my true self can explore. And central to my vocation and my life's work is to help create similar communities through circles, dialogue, and the written word.

Ultimately, it is in places where we gather that we share a responsibility to encourage and explore true community together.

You will know when you are in true community because it will invite you to develop a true sense of self; it will encourage you to explore who you are. There will be a natural receiving and giving, a deep sense of hospitality, listening and sharing, and a place where you can explore your desire to take risks.

Where community is lost, like among many who support the current Trump administration and invite division and cruelty, participants lose touch with their humanity. A further fragmentation takes place, and those in these false communities generate an epidemic of hungry ghosts.

As a Buddhist practitioner, I understand now that there is no enlightenment, no spiritual epiphany without the other, without community. Our spiritual life is a communal one, whether that is consciously acknowledged or not. We truly are in this together.

> *A Dhammic community, then, is a community based on the fundamental equality of all beings that both affirms and transcends all distinctions, be they gender, ethnicity, or class. Such a view does not deny the existence of differences among individuals or groups. But all people, regardless of position and status, should understand that their own personal well-being depends on the well-being of all.*
>
> —Buddhadasa Bhikkhu, *Heartwood of the Bodhi Tree*

FOSTERING TRUE COMMUNITY

The subtitle of Parker's book *A Hidden Wholeness* is "Welcoming the soul and weaving community in a wounded world." True community, as both John McKnight and Parker point out, isn't so much something we invent or design, but something we join in and help foster, something we weave together. I enjoyed listening to John at his book talk as he named the hallmarks and inherent qualities of an abundant community: "contribution, gifts, a welcoming of strangers, interactive, and the mysterious."

To foster true community, all we have to do is continue to explore what true community is for us. To realize true community, we can use the **Inner Labyrinth** from Chapter One as a template to explore what community means. To foster community is to openly explore it; to explore community means to realize and express our own true nature within it.

Ask yourself: *Where have you felt safe and authentic? What was taking place in this setting that encouraged your true self to emerge? How might you receive true community? Where do you come alive? To whom and what do you belong?*

LIFE FOLLOWS OUR GAZE: FINDING THE ABUNDANCE

When I catch myself struggling in relationships, I find that I may be caught up in what I am not getting, what is not working, and focusing in on what I don't want. In reality, when we meet the "other" we are always meeting our self. To receive the other is to receive our self. And in all of the relationships we have chosen to remain in, there will be qualities about the other that rub us the wrong way. I am pointing to struggles that arise between you and others whom you have chosen to be in relationship with. I am not in any way suggesting that you remain in toxic, neglectful, or abusive relationships or environments. In fact, perhaps the time has come to rethink these relationships and your involvement in them.

Our attention is like a superpower that can be misused to divide us, or as an instrument to unite us. Life, as it turns out, follows our gaze.

TRY THIS: WHERE IS YOUR ATTENTION?

On entering any new place we can use the pithy practice of the Three R's (page 63). You can explore these questions yourself or you can help a group explore them together. What is our community about? What is this gathering about? In true community, we understand there are difficulties and challenges. These may even be what brought us together. But in true community we focus on the gifts that can be received and given.

A horse trainer once reminded me that a horse will go in the direction of the rider's gaze. Rather than tugging on the reins, shouting at the horse, or kicking it, all I have to do is look in the direction I want the horse to go while gently leaning in that same direction. Mind you, I tested this approach out for myself. The horse could sense my lack of experience, I am sure. So as I sat stiff and doubtful, my trainer invited me to relax. "Breathe, Julie, and as you gently tug on the reins, gaze and lean in the direction you want the horse to go." I took some breaths, silenced my busy mind, and gazed to the right. And the horse obediently followed my gaze and started to move in that direction.

The most profound influence that determines and directs our individual and collective experience is where we hold our gaze. Wherever we place our attention, our leanings, there our energy and efforts will go. We have to hold our gaze softly "ahead" to where we want to go so our collective lives move in a forward direction. We also want to focus on our gifts, as well as the gifts of others. So, unlike focusing on the negatives, we give our attention to what is possible: *What am I getting, what is working, and what do I want.*

Can we offer up our attention to others as a gift to be given, rather than tightly holding onto our opinions like reins on a horse?

If our life seems like an unresponsive horse, we can turn our gaze forward and focus on the gifts available to us while navigating the particulars of each moment. Breathe, notice where your attention or the group's attention is in any given moment, and then help redirect the focus if necessary.

FINDING A TRUE SPIRITUAL COMMUNITY

> *In order for us to develop some roots, we need the kind of environment that can help us become rooted. A sangha is not a community of practice in which each person is an island, unable to communicate with each other—this is not a true sangha. No healing or transformation will result from such a sangha. A true sangha should be like a family in which there is a spirit of brotherhood and sisterhood.*
>
> —Thich Nhat Hanh, *Friends on the Path: Living Spiritual Communities*

Here I offer us some words from this book's poet Rebecca Cecchini, who is an active leader in the Dominican community:

Too often we look for our "place," want to confirm who we are, and identify our community, by way of deciding what we are not or, more specifically, what is not us. And so the debilitating "us and not us" framework is born in our minds, and entrenches itself in every aspect of our lives.

Though we might have fumbled our way to grasping the truth that all is connected, and all is therefore "in belonging," belonging is not simple. Belonging is dynamic, dependent, complex. It is vulnerable and fragile too—and we still struggle to comprehend belonging at the most basic of levels.

But belonging is the truth of this life—all life in this mansion of many rooms. When felt, it is the seat of our joy. When understood and prized, it is the foundation of our intentional practices of laying down our gifts beside others in communities. When together, and on our varied paths, we mirror this truth that all is wholly in belonging, a holy presence reveals itself. At least in part.

Too often, using our "us and not us" framework, one gift is seen as a challenge to another, rather than a prized element of our intrinsic diversity. Then our heart to heart communications get forced underground, into heart, to the safety of the inviolable realm of individual conscience and consciousness, where we listen for our truth. This, our sanctuary for true dialogue with divine nature (our own, and the greater) is essential to our being, literally a saving grace. But it's not to be our soul's permanent shelter. Not one thing in our known universe exists, much less thrives, by separation. And our individual presence is not meant to stay put in internal retreat and dialogue. We must always emerge again into active relationship. Hopefully bringing back to the conversations our truths discerned in the deep. No matter if we would choose this reality or not, relationship is where we live and have our being.

Spiritual communities bear a great responsibility to provide safe, encouraging, welcoming support. To not stifle a soul's efforts at becoming, we need to prize the softness of a heart, as much as we do the conviction of another. What though, when we are committed to our spiritual community, and that community fails its larger responsibility to create a strong enough, flexible enough framework to hold all of its parts and receive the benefit of their gifts? What happens when those entrusted with leadership, wearing the mantle of legitimacy, fail their task of service? Each individual understanding of place in community is jeopardized. Gifts are not brought forth. Some will pass, untapped.

A spiritual community makes a mistake to presume it knows and has defined, once and for all, its own form and manner of functioning. In the same way each of us evolves in self-knowledge, awareness, sense of purpose, and connectedness to others, so must any (living) spiritual community continue to form and reform for the sake and care of the life of the spirit it means to serve. That means continuously making room for all the gifts—not just those that are known, but for what is still hidden, suppressed, or denied. There must be room for wonder, surprise, disappointment, failings, and forgiveness. There must be room to correct misperceptions. There must always be gentleness, and room to learn. Yes we must value learning. Else our stores of wonder have all been spent, all the answers procured for all time (and so far no one has told me this is so). Thriving communities are so, when they continue to become more fully reflective and inclusive of their whole, when they respect each part and each discovery for what it brings, and when they can be hospitable to what rises and challenges their most precious, deep-set notions.

We find ourselves these days in a time of transition in our spiritual and social realms—trying to read the signs, trying to listen, wondering what happened to our clear vision of where we (thought we) were headed. Many in our world are hearing the message that their gifts are not wanted. That in fact, they have not gifts. This is us failing one another. This is us failing ourselves.

We are, every one of us, called to consciousness and the recognition of our belonging. Called to preach with word and action, the Love that asks mercy—not sacrifice, and binds all. We are called to intentionally be mind, or heart, or hands—strength, and support in concert with all parts of the body which, in its very existence, reflects the Holy. All is contained in the connective presence of the Holy. All is wholly in belonging.

Well beyond recognition of belonging, the real invitation of Spirit is to communion. And I am to make my way there in the good company and support of others awaiting and echoing my yes with their own acceptances in communion—a community of communities.

I do not know entirely how I will answer this invitation for my part, or even what could possibly make for an adequate reply to the announcement of such blessing. Though I think that when my yes looks half as grand as a blade of grass that, in growing to become its simple true self, sings its own praise of Life inherent in the wild chorus of other greening—and so becomes the Alleluia—I will have answered that call.

TRY THIS: REFRAMING COMMUNITY

If we need to, we can readjust our understanding of community and, therefore, our experience of it. In this case it may be helpful to identify an old story of community and then reframe it with a new story—a newly emerging narrative. My reframe of community has been ongoing, and this is a good thing. Our narratives about what community is, or what anything is for that matter, must be kept in the eternal conversation and not become false or stagnant. We need to take responsibility for cultivating communities where the soul can be fully present. Again the emphasis is on generosity and hospitality.

There are many types of communities: the spiritual, the therapeutic, the civic, the identity group (gender, race, ethnicity), the vocational, and the organizational. All have universal qualities that make for a true community, such as the inclusive hospitality offered to each other's differences and gifts.

Just as we did in the previous chapter, here we can reframe our understanding of community. We can explore both individually and collectively the old frame of a given community and its possible new frame. At some point, if the community is to share its gifts, all of its members must be able and willing to reframe its intentions and purposes together. I reframed my experience with my sangha on my latest return to that community. However, without the hospitality on their end, without receptivity to shaping our community together, a solo reframe was not going to generate any movement within that particular setting. So begin with yourself. Begin to reframe community, or a particular community, and then invite others to join in with you.

First, write out your old story of community—the old way you frame community—by writing out its narrative. Then write the new narrative(s). When doing this with others you can use a chalkboard and draw out the narratives. Do your best to come up with four key narratives that lend to a positive reframe of community, thereby inviting the gifts and possibilities of each and all. The reframe isn't about solving problems or what to do about this or that. Rather, it is about how we view community and what individual and shared stories we carry within us about that community. These narratives direct our gaze and our actions. And our abundance becomes visible through the welcoming of each other, the dialogue around our reframes, and the exchange of our past and present stories.

TRICKIER THAN BREATHING

One fundamental quality of true community is our ability to be in silence together, to be able to frame community and solitude as compatible and necessary partners. I began my seminar for my university students with a poem and then three minutes of silence. I start my therapy sessions with a shared silence, often awkward moments—encouraging a shared solitude. In therapy, it is so important for the therapist not to rush in and fill in and direct the start of a session. Instead this space and silence allows for the client to listen and know what she wants to share. We often want to fill up awkward moments of silence when in these shared spaces something more real can and will emerge.

Solitude has a deep and valuable part in true community. As long as we maintain an awareness of our inner makings and leanings, which are dependent on times of solitude and contemplation, we will experience true community. However, bringing our true selves into community, honoring the other, while receiving the gifts of community are trickier than breathing. But as necessary as the air we share and breathe.

JOIN IN AND COME AS YOU ARE

My daughter attended a weekend leadership course called Freshman Connection. Its intention was to help new students connect and find ways to claim leadership roles in their upcoming new community of campus life. During the weekend a few TED Talks were screened. One of them, "How to Start a Movement" by Derek Sivers, revealed how movements get started. Someone starts dancing alone among a crowd of people sitting at a park. Then someone else gets up—the first "follower"—and dances with the identified "leader" who started the dance. Once the second person has joined in, others tend to rapidly do so also.

Who are the leaders here? The message of this talk was that the community of dancers would not have happened if it weren't for the second person, who took a risk by joining in with the solo dancer. "The first follower is an underestimated form of leadership. It takes guts to stand out like that. The first follower is what takes a lone nut and transforms him or her into a leader."

Although the person who started the dance alone will be the recognized leader, in my view the first follower (the second participant in the dance) is the true leader. Again, "new followers emulate the followers, not the leader." Soon a tipping point results and ergo! We have a crowd of dancers, a community of movers. Derek Sivers points out that the greater the number of dancers, the less risky it becomes to join in. In fact, at a certain point, it may become more uncomfortable to sit out than to join in.

I have sometimes thought that in order to lead I had to be the first, the smartest, or the loudest. I thought I had to stand out to make a difference. Now I look around me for the opportunity to join in, as the second participant or the even the last, as a way to co-create true community and to be part of the larger dance.

And in circles where I am the designated leader, I send out this invitation, one that I go on to remind people about throughout our time together: *Come as you are with what you have*. I trust the gifts of community will arrive too as we gather, and know that each person will bring what they want and choose to our gatherings.

We are each teacher and student, in the exchange of ideas and stories. I may be the "designated facilitator," but it is the rest of those attending that leads us all into a shared dance. In Parker's writings and teachings on circles of trust, the group facilitator of such circles is an "engaged facilitator"—one that arrives and participates but doesn't stand apart from the process. Even as a teacher, I know I am learning as I teach. When we separate ourselves out from the class or circle, we are encouraging a false sense of community, and it is not leading through example. In the end the group and us as leader will be undermined. Nature continually points to how we are always in this together, always in community with one another, always sharing our resources and knowledge. This participating in community through leadership is what the next chapter is about.

Come as you are is a timely reminder about how to best participate in our true communities. We invite ourselves to explore what is possible and come as we are with the gifts we have to offer. Sometimes the gift is our grief or anxiety, sometimes it is a simple question, and sometimes it is a song or poem. Come; come, as you are, the more the merrier.

> **Who held the light aloft for your eyes**
> **was clear to you—you were sure.**
> **Had been for a long time.**
> **But Another stands behind that torch bearer, unseen**
> **until your eyes are ready, or another draws them**
> **to the truth. That One too, was always there.**
>
> **Don't mind that others saw this all along.**
>
> **It wasn't their fate, bore a different weight**
> **to the eyes of their souls. That vision was fated**
> **to come to you, an engraved invitation,**
> **to enter into service as your heart was cast to**
> **bear its light, further, forward**
> **in the life of the Spirit.**

CHAPTER NINE

HANDING OTHERS THE RED THREAD: LEADERSHIP AS EVERYONE'S VOCATION

> *Leadership is a concept we often resist. It seems immodest, even self-aggrandizing, to think ourselves as leaders. But if it is true that we are part of a community, then leadership is everyone's vocation, and it can be an evasion to insist that it is not. When we live in the close-knit ecosystem called community, everyone follows and everyone leads.*
>
> —Parker J. Palmer

LEARNING TO BE LEFT BEHIND

In most versions of the myth, Theseus abandons Ariadne once he is out of the labyrinth. For our purposes, Ariadne represents the leader who first gifts Theseus with the ball of red thread. Such a gift! It is magnificent and ultimately saves his life. Still, he leaves her on the shore asleep as he returns home by ship.

We want to be the teachers and leaders that are left behind. That is what this chapter is about: leading with integrity as we pass the red thread on to others. We also want to be the leaders as citizens who keep hold of the red thread in our own lives. (This is what the next and final chapter is about: rejoining soul in the roles we live.)

The betrayal—when Ariadne is abandoned by the one she has helped—happens to each of us at some point as we become the ones who pass on the red thread. In point of fact, we should be abandoned by our students or followers (and adult children) as they fall in love with the world and become leaders and citizens themselves. In our leadings and teachings we help the person fall in love with the gifts, not the giver. This is how we give back to those who have helped us in some way: we integrate their teachings in a personal way that matters in the real world. The truest leaders bring forth and honor the teacher and leader in the other.[9]

On my last visit with Parker, I felt the glow of a valuable awareness: in our relationship I was the student, a student he saw as a teacher for others. For my part, I experienced myself as more student than teacher. But I know, too, that he honored fully my inner teacher and the teacher I am in the world. I was and am deeply grateful for his hospitality toward me. I know, too, that he benefited from my hospitality. This hospitality included my receiving these conversations from him. The hospitality was also in my giving back to him in our conversations and in the writing of this book.

How important it is for all of us to be able to be both student and teacher, follower and leader. If I kept myself always a student in my relationship with Parker, I would come to depend too heavily on Parker the man and rely on outside circumstances to continually teach and define me. And, for those of us who see ourselves always as teacher (therapist, leader), we can become isolated and trapped by keeping ourselves divided from others and, in some cases, wrongly "above" others. We also keep a divide within ourselves. I mentioned in the previous chapter how we can hide behind our various leadership roles (teacher, mother, counselor). The best teachers and leaders are able to sit at the foot of another and learn.

As I interpret true Buddhist tradition, the best teachers are in fact forgotten because the teachings are so alive and strong in the student's heart, mind, and actions that they forget the teacher. The student is so focused on what they receive and on the forward motion of their life, they forget the one who gifted them. This may seem dramatic, but we should all be aiming for our students, clients, and anyone else we may be leading, such as our children, to gain access to their inner teacher that knows what they need and want. What we want for someone else, no matter how worthy, is always mixed up in our own histories and narrative. We must let go of what we want for the other and trust their capacities to explore and discover on their own.

WE ARE ALL LEADERS, ALWAYS LEADING

In every moment of our life, we set an example and make a statement about who we are. And *the central responsibility of a leader is to consciously and purposefully set an example of how to be a whole human being.*

As leaders, it is essential to keep our spiritual teachings and explorations personal and close. That means to not just think about the teachings, instead, as we lead from within, we engage in an internal conversation with all that is arising in us and about us. As I have shared, I was raised in an alcoholic, dysfunctional family environment that extended its tentacles to cousins, aunts, uncles, neighbors, and friends. Therefore, I learned certain "unrealities" about the world, which I am still unlearning. When I think I am done with my inner work, spirit shows up with an opportunity to wake me up to reality. Reality is sanity; sanity is feeling our belonging and not being bossed around by our habitual patterns built into us by our histories. But it can be a challenge to know what our patterns are—especially when we're in them—and to know what exactly is contributing to our suffering. That is the valuable work of exploring a dynamic: discovering and transforming what causes us to suffer.

As a writer there is a danger that I will figure everything out on paper but not extend this consciousness beyond the written word. That is the reason for creating and attending places—such as circles of trust—where the soul can be heard, especially places where you can hear your own soul's wisdom. Sometimes inner wisdom comes through what you share; sometimes it comes through what someone else reveals. Your inner voice can also come through the teachings, for example red thread, twelve-step, zero point. These shared places for the soul help us go deep without frightening ourselves off the spiritual and exploratory path.

Earlier I shared how I once didn't trust my own capacity to

navigate a new time in my life. This new time was marked by the empty nest, my partner at the time's retirement, my approaching sixtieth birthday, and a friend's illness. In a group dialogue with my teacher Santikaro, I was able to notice my doubts and then tap into my capacity to move into my (reframed) second adulthood. Now, through a conversation with a friend who has been in Al-Anon for years, I discovered how I have distrusted the capacity of others for nearly my entire life. Think how this limits my leading! I had learned early on in life that others don't have the capacity to stop drinking, to make healthy choices, or to rely on a spiritual or psychological path. This, of course, influenced how I parented and led.

This doubting influenced every relationship to different degrees. And it burdened me. The only way I discovered this was through a soulful friendship and attending Al-Anon meetings. I joined Al-Anon (about four decades late, but hey—better late than never!).

At this juncture I became ready and willing to act as if I trusted everyone's capacity, fully, especially those close in. I frame it as "act as if," knowing that the habitual feelings and doubts will arise, as they are part of my family legacy. When they do I can host the edge and focus on reality—a reality that assures me I can fully trust the other's capacity to find their own way. Now, as the mother of an adult daughter, and as a teacher, counselor, leader, and spiritual friend, I do my best to trust more fully the other's capacity, especially when it comes to difficult challenges. This was a pivotal quickening for me. This was a renewal and strengthening of trusting others further, back to where this book began—my blind dog and Parker trusting me and how this trust allowed for true generosity and hospitality between us.

However, this particular dynamic may not be part of your history, your story, or your inner leanings. You may have been thinking when reading the above story: *I trust others' capacities over my own!* We each are unique. That is the reason inner work must be personal and not dictated by some outside institution, teacher, or program. We all share in one reality: we lead from within either consciously or unconsciously. So it takes a continual effort and contemplation to maintain an awakened way of living and leading from within.

Again, it all comes back to trust. This book happened because

Parker extended his total trust in me. "I totally trust you, Julie." Not surprising that we often come around to some core teachings that help us to cross over one rushing river after another.

> **Hope**
> **used to come first to mind—was first off my tongue,**
> **as though I knew its form,**
> **could wave its light like a torch**
> **in front of my feet.**
> **This dark, close air of *wonder when?***
> **is testing my vision.**

WHEN CROSSING A RUSHING RIVER

When opportunities arise as leaders that shake our own footing, it is best to find a respectful pace that takes you across to the other side. As leaders this can't be about performance or perfection. We must remain inwardly directed. For me, the passage was much like crossing a rushing river. Trusting another's capacity to handle the consequences of my choices was, and still can be, rough going. After all, I had lived a part of my life believing that I had to do certain things and take on certain choices because others couldn't handle it if I made a choice that would affect them in challenging, possibly painful, ways.

And when we are crossing a rushing river there are always others witnessing. We are always leading and setting an example for someone. As a parent I am always teaching my daughter. In our acknowledgment as leaders we experience the paradox of crossing for ourselves and showing others how it can be done. Again, even as I write this, I fully know it all to be true in my heart and in my head. My responsibility now as a conscious human being is to continue to attend to this new, emerging reality.

When crossing rushing rivers of your own, don't hurry. Find a pace that works for you. Do your best not to force actions on yourself or others. And while crossing the river, which is mostly if not entirely internal, find your unique pace, but don't stop. At a recent teaching, Santikaro spoke about the benefits of twelve-step and how one in this program is committed, having learned the hard way that the spiritual practice is a matter of life and death. Why waiver? He used the word dawdling. Why dawdle? Yes, go at our own pace but don't dawdle. Keep taking one step at a time until you are on the other side. Don't make any major decisions or force others to follow you in any way. Then invite others across when you feel your own feet on solid ground.

A woman came to the Buddha asking for guidance. She mentioned how she was always fumbling and asked how to do better in her life. The Buddha simply recommended that she "fumble forward."

WHAT TO DO ONCE ON THE OTHER SIDE (OF THE RUSHING WATER)

Once we obtain some wisdom and leadership, we don't necessarily serve our community best by creating some program, new religion, or retreat. All we need is to continue to show up as we are. Be ourselves. Keep fumbling forward and climbing hills, setting examples as we go.

As my daughter and I drove through southern Ireland, with the help of a GPS we found places that were hidden treasures, such as Uragh Stone Circle. This place is not in the tourist books. There were no road signs along the way, only one small, hand-painted sign next to the walking path to the stones. We had to stop many times and ask for directions. There were no gates. The roads were too small for tourist buses or SUVs.

Once we had arrived, I found this to be one of the most beautiful sights I had visited in my lifetime. Conscious citizens and leaders are like this stone circle. Hidden, but here. We don't need a lot of hoopla and road signs for our students or visitors to find us. Our students and visitors will find us—though it helps to be willing to ask for directions.

In a previous chapter, I disclosed how I once had received the "right" book inside a different book cover. This is what I want to say about that: Life is full of pivotal moments when our conversation with divinity and destiny occur. The thing is, the conversations are unique to each of us but are not proof that "this" is the right book or method for anyone else. We've all seen how, down through time, some powerful spiritual/psychological experiences have been turned into a transformational program or even a religion. Many psychological scams and cults are built on true-life experiences. Methods of transformation and teaching are tools to have handy in our tool kit. However, one size will never fit all when it comes to discovering meaning or making a difference in the world.

Authentic leaders use personal spiritual experiences to open up more to our own divinity and destiny; authentic leaders don't design programs that encourage conversion experiences, bring in big bucks, or attract blind-faith devotees. Too often I have seen people have a conversion experience of their own, and the first thing they want to do is go out and recruit or teach others. True leaders set an example and share what works but don't insist or imply that theirs is the only way. Agendas and expectations are not pushed onto others who have come seeking guidance.

We "see what works" through dialogue. Together we explore and share methods, but the emphasis is on conversation and exploration. Leaders who lead with integrity encourage others to honor their own inner knowing. Having had a direct spiritual experience of meaning, we may get enthused by some cause. Then, we go about sharing this enthusiasm with others as an invitation. The best leaders are in a dialogue wherein they are receptive to new discoveries about themselves and the world.

BECOMING TREASURE REVEALERS

In a healthy, dynamic family, a child is born and the parents understand that their job is to help their child become who they are intended to become. Parents' role is to help their child explore their destiny. The parents will mirror their child, as a way to host their loved one's natural enfoldment of self. The mirror itself is a neutral presence not reflecting itself onto the other but letting the child, the other, be seen in them! Reflected in this mirror are the child's true nature and capabilities and potentialities.

In an unhealthy, nondynamic family, a child is born and the parents assume—consciously or not— that their child exists to fulfill their needs, to make them happy. Their child is there to help them to fulfill their destiny. They are not able to reflect back; instead, they project themselves onto their child. This projection includes their hopes and fears, their unmet dreams, and the images and identities they want to show the world. I can only claim that I consciously chose to be a treasure revealer, a mirror for my daughter, as best I could. However, I know there were intersections in our shared life where I projected my fears and hopes onto her. I have caught myself wanting her to be a certain way that clearly satisfies my needs, not hers.

In our desire to be the best parent, teacher, or leader we can be, we want to do our best to be mirrors to others, to be treasure revealers, to help others explore their possibilities and potentialities. We have a huge impact and influence on those who rely on our guidance and ways. We must work hard to do our best.

When, as children, we are not mirrored, as too many of us have not been, we are encouraged to become "like our parents" or to please them in some way. Later in life, many of us rebel, only to do everything we can to not become like our parents, but still not fulfilling our own personal destinies. So again, our role as leaders and teachers is to become better mirrors for others, to become treasure revealers.

The movie *Guess Who's Coming to Dinner*, which starred Sidney Poitier, is a great example of how our adult children and students don't owe us anything. A favorite scene of mine is when Poitier, playing the fiancé, confronts his father with his intentions of marrying a white girl. The father, who is opposed to this plan, reminds the son how much he and his mother have sacrificed for him. The son reminds the father that he owes him nothing for doing what a father is supposed to do.

As leaders, we want to hold ourselves accountable. It's not a small requirement to be willing to be left behind like Adriadne and then to not constantly project our selves onto those around us. However, the benefits of such efforts are often miraculous and always felt. Most people come into my circles and sessions with a serious lack of mirroring or the ability to explore ideas for themselves. They often don't know what they want but are clear about what others want of them. Through conversation, mirroring, and exploration, profound transformation takes place.

YOU AS TERTON

When mirroring and helping others explore for themselves, we become the other's Terton, which in Tibetan means "a treasure revealer." Tertons are those who can see and hear beyond their own illusions and projections and so are able to reveal others' treasures to them. (Historically, secret texts, called *terma* in Tibetan, were hidden until such a time that their treasures could be revealed to those ready for such knowledge. But we are all ready! We have always been ready to be mirrored and to mirror). As a Terton we can help open others up to their inner hidden treasures through conversation, asking the right questions, sharing poetry and stories, and mirroring back to them.

As leaders, we are asked to see beyond our own projections and demands and be hospitable to the other, as best we can. So my and your willingness to stay ever alert to our own shadow self and live and lead in touch with our inner callings, is being a Terton.

To help others explore and to be a treasure revealer we must hold a discipline ourselves to do so. Let me be honest—it takes discipline not to take credit for something. Our ego wants the outward appreciation and validation for what we have accomplished. It takes discipline to be the second or third one joining in and leading in this way, instead of being a recognized leader. I have noticed that even the more introverted leaders who may often go last and follow, still feel disappointed when not recognized for their courage and achievements. This desire to be recognized, appreciated, and applauded is only human, and is the reason it takes discipline to set this yearning aside. The truly courageous leader is the one who does the inner work to move out beyond such egoistic leanings. Some leaders are less inclined to wanting such alkaloids from their achievements, the various Mandelas and Dalai Lamas among us. I am not one of them. I may at times find myself getting nudged when someone gets applauded and rewarded for something that I, too, have brought to the world. I take a deep breath, host this edge, and then rely on various disciplines to help me lead from within. There are those, too, who are hungry ghosts actually feeding off the approval and admiration of others.

When I was thirteen, I gave up marijuana. I had signed up

for a seminar to learn Transcendental Meditation. There was the promise and therefore the motivation to feel at peace, and the possibility to attain enlightenment. Who would pass up such an opportunity? The catch was that they asked us to abstain from marijuana for up to thirty days so that the THC it contained would not be in our system. They claimed—and research backed them up—that we would not be able to receive the benefits of meditation if we were high in any way. Therefore, we would not be given the mantra until we were THC-free.

This was the opportunity to give up pot that I was actually looking for—to give up pot and maybe, just maybe, find a way to be at peace with myself and my surroundings. The ease it took to throw the remaining hashish I had down the toilet pointed to my motivation to be free, to know more at peace, and to be part of something larger than myself. I never smoked marijuana again.

This is what authentic leadership is like: We are deeply motivated by some inner callings that make the discipline of leadership seem effortless. And we experience the rewards internally; we tap into a sort of sanity when doing the right thing. And this "thing" always makes us more whole. Outwardly, everyone who comes in contact with us is thusly rewarded.

Then out beyond this choice of not getting high and starting meditation is my next choice, my next hill to climb or rushing waters to cross. I have wavered and wandered from these inner knowings at times. And I may again. But I know what to return to—this inner dialogue with my soul's leanings and callings. And when I listen and make choices motivated by this inner dialogue, I am always led, and lead others, to a place of shared discoveries. As long as I can discipline myself to check in with the motivations behind my choices, my leadings will be of benefit.

> **Ordinary strides
> up a sunlit hill of a humdrum day,
> but something shadowy and fast
> passed through those woods.
> In case I forgot,
> no walk is ordinary,
> or alone.**

WHAT MOTIVATES YOU?

What motivates you to lead or teach in this particular situation? What do you hope to get out of it? Is this motivation internally or externally driven? Or both? Of course, we want to positively impact the outer world, and this is an outward manifestation of our inner motivation. However, does this easily segue into a reliance on needing to be recognized as the leader or for any related achievements? Are you trying to recruit or persuade people to your way of thinking? Or is your motivation driven from a place of belonging and community?

Throughout this book I have pointed to many disciplines that invite our true self and encourage true community and leadership:

- Being able to receive in order to give
- Exploration/beginner's mind
- Naming our dynamics
- Identifying antidotes
- The promise of paradox (both-and)
- The ability to be in solitude
- A willingness to be contemplative
- Hosting ours edges (and those of others)
- The eternal conversation
- Asking the beautiful question
- Generosity and hospitality
- Use of a third thing, like poetry
- Living consciously from our side of a conversation (Zero Point Agreement)

HOSTING OTHERS' EDGES

As we become better hosts of our own edges, we are ready to help host the edges of others. Of course, this doesn't mean we host theirs for them, but we become a host to their edges in a way that allows them to host their own. This is the nature of hospitality and "being at home" with ourselves and others. Hosting does not interfere with the other's explorations but offers a presence of heart and soul as the other goes inward.[10] A teacher of mine once said that we have to allow our children to experience the effects of their lives. We can't follow them around protecting them from the disappointments and pain of life. We have to let them figure out for themselves how to respond to difficulty and how to handle disappointment. I nodded my head in agreement. Now, a couple decades later as a mom of a young adult, I realize that even in situations where she asks me to be involved, it is important that I do so in a way that doesn't violate her personal integrity.

I witness parents who rescue their adult children from financial and personal ruin again and again. The adult children never quite experience the full consequences of their choices and mistakes and so never learn the ability to transform difficulty into opportunity. Often these adult children find someone else to rely upon, usually someone who is drawn to codependent relationships. Unfortunately, there are times it seems that our world is strewn with suffering and difficulty, and there are no solutions readily available. My heart breaks a little every day witnessing all the pain in the world. I do my best not to add to the suffering. I do my best to be part of the solution instead of adding to the problem. I act in ways that demonstrate to my daughter how an adult responds to difficulty and let her navigate the rushing waters and hills of her life.

One approach that helps me lead from within is to have reminders. These reminders can come in the form of pithy slogans, an inspirational quote, or a short list. Here I offer up eight reminders that have helped me lead from within, to be fearless and compassionate as I pass on the red thread. You may use these or create your own.

The Eight Reminders to True Leadership:
How to Pass On the Red Thread

1. *Know how to follow.* Allow ourselves to be led and taught by others, as well as by third things such as consultations with the *I Ching* or reading poetry. Each day spend time "following" another's wisdom or your higher power's nudging. In public situations, consider how you can join in to help the cause.

2. *Mutual influence is the fundamental foundation, the hallmark to healthy, dynamic relationships and to each conversation*

within our relationships. Marriages, friendships, and work relationships are all dependent upon this quality. Mutual influence depends on both people in the conversation being ethical, truthful, and open. A willingness to be influenced is dependent upon a vulnerability and curiosity toward the other, a genuine motivation to understand the other and then be influenced by what the other has to say. Both Gottman's research on successful and happy heterosexual marriages as well as the five-thousand-year-old philosophy of the *I Ching* highlight that our ability to be influenced by the other is critical for flourishing relationships. Mutual influence is dependent upon some level of respect and vulnerability with each other. In Gottman's studies of good marriages, he refers to it as "allowing for influence." Because he studied only heterosexual couples, he emphasized how the male needs to let himself be influenced by the woman because he believes this quality is more natural for women. I find in my work within organizations that difficulty often arises when the leaders or employers (deans, bosses, supervisors, directors) are not open to mutual influence. They hold the expectation of influencing others but lack the skill of mutuality. The root of all relationships, even with your spiritual source, needs to be of mutual influence—give and take; back and forth. Mutual means an authentic receptivity to the other. Influence means that we allow for ourselves to be impacted by the other.

This influence is felt and shown out in the open too. Wherever there is difficulty in relationships, there is likely a lack of mutual influence. To generate a mutual influence you must focus on opening your heart to the other through listening and understanding and then allowing yourself to be altered by the other. This encourages a genuine curiosity about the other—their stories, experiences, and ideas. It is through this mutual influence that we truly benefit ourselves and others. A mutual influence happens when you let your heart be moved by the other. Of course, the word mutual implies that both individuals are invested in this exchange of influence. However, you can practice allowing yourself to be influenced by the other, and this may transform any rigidity in the relationship. Many people tell me how a successful practice of this does wonders for their relationships with their teenagers. This mutual influence is felt by the young adult and builds their confidence.

3. **Live the Zero Point Agreement.** Live life from our own side, taking full responsibility for our experiences. Live consciously from the inside out, and create ways to encourage this in others.

4. **We consistently host our own edges, which includes relying on our ethical and spiritual principles to guide us through challenging times with others.**

5. **We have a regular practice through which we contemplate and study our principles, and explore through journal writing.** The motivation is to keep our life conscious and honest with a clear hearing to true self.

6. **We do our best not to hold the past against our self, or others.** This means to host the present not the past. Of course, this is far more easily said then done, but I hold on to this as a way to be with others. Our past agreements and beliefs and our supporting assumptions based on our history prevent us from taking risks, reaching out, and making something remarkable happen. I refer to these as the pain stories we carry around with us. Up until now you may have been using much of your energy (consciously and unconsciously) to perpetuate your pain stories, your past. In these stories, we carry around assumptions about why things are the way they are and why we need what we need, as well as our assumptions about everything and everyone. Our pain stories may have originated with acerbic events, but we are the playwright of our lives now (and the director and actor). Therefore, the historical and conditional cause of any particular pain story holds no power in comparison to our ability to reframe and re-create our lives. When in agreement with the past, we keep projecting the past onto the present. We live from the past, seeing and creating it over and over again.

Many people ask, "Why does this keep happening to me?" when the questions would best be: "What do I do to contribute to this pattern again and again?" and "What can I do to interfere with this pattern and create a new story for myself?" One doesn't need a therapist to be free from the past. One needs the tools—sometimes afforded through therapy—that allow you to be aware of your pain story, along with a willingness to practice living life actively and ethically from your side.

7. *Do our best to meet others and circumstances halfway.* Gandhi came to believe and then demonstrate that any ability he had to improve upon the world around him occurred when he got out of his own way—when he met the world around him halfway and "emptied" himself out. He referred to this as "reducing yourself to zero." Showing up halfway means respecting the personal boundaries and integrity in all relationships. To show up halfway we have to become aware of this halfway position in our relationships. We want to be able to find this halfway point and live our life there with others. I encourage my clients to locate this halfway mark in their relationships by imagining an invisible line between them and the other—and then to notice when or how they are crossing over the boundary. Ask yourself, Where is this place in my relationships and communications with others? What does it look like to go past halfway? What does it look like to hang back from this meeting place? Hanging back means you are isolating yourself or are not truly committed to that particular relationship. There can be no communication or intimacy with "the other" if we are not meeting them halfway

We can also make the mistake of going past the halfway mark in our relationships. When we go past halfway we are typically being codependent, crossing personal boundaries, and doing or taking on too much. In these relationships you may find yourself resenting the other, getting overwhelmed with responsibilities until you become exhausted. We also tend to go past halfway when we do not trust the other to show up.

It is better to wait at the halfway point than to cross the boundary to try to get what you want. Live your life from your side at this halfway place and notice who shows up. You will find this principle in the *I Ching* as well, where we are guided to meet even the Creator halfway. In relationship with your spiritual source, not showing up halfway means you are not in an active relationship with this source. How do you expect to experience sacred connection when you hold yourself back? When we go past halfway in our relationship to our spiritual source we don't allow room for the Great Unknown to help us. A way to identify this "halfway point" is to create solitude in our relationships and gatherings.

8. ***Listen for and share story.*** When encountering others, and when leading, there is always a story. In my first book, Hidden Victims Hidden Healers: An Eight-Stage Healing Process for Family and Friends of the Mentally Ill, the first stage is to write and share your story with others in order to grasp an understanding about how another's mental illness has impacted us. When meeting up with others, we listen for their story. What story as a group or community are we living by or wanting to change? What teaching story can we use, as a third thing, to add or to reframe our individual or collective stories? In all my circles, participants have an evening where they can share some of their pain stories with others. In reality, all conversation is story. Our stories are clues, a red thread, that contain insight to who we truly are and what we are truly capable of. And when listening to another's story, here is an opportunity to mirror the other, to be a Treasure Revealer.

HOW BIG CAN WE GET: HOW FEARLESS CAN WE BE?

I have encountered and written much about false teachers and shamans. My work is mainly about helping others lead but includes what to do when we encounter a harmful teacher, counselor, psychic, leader, shaman, guru, etc. Just recently, in my research for this chapter, I came upon yet another well-known spiritual teacher, whom I studied under, utterly lacking

> **Eyes that held the greening of six million years,**
> **teeth that never straightened in all that time**
> **(better things to work on—wit for instance),**
> **were not the real fierceness**
> **that old croc flashed at me.**
>
> ***You're not being grateful***
> ***for ways being made,*** **says he,** *if you do not*
> ***bring the gifts on ahead.***

in integrity and who consistently acted out of the shadow self. This particular teacher and leader gets away with a myriad of abuses because too many followers are seduced and captured by his charisma and fame. He dictates what the student/teacher relationship should be if they want to have access to "the" (his!) teachings. The teachings are authentic, and in reality, in the public domain. He is passing down teachings that have been available for thousands of years.

This is a sure warning sign of a false and shadowy teacher—a claim of special access to the teachings of the Buddha, Jesus, or God. This teacher's students forget that he cannot claim to know the one and only way to get into the kingdom of God, become enlightened, or achieve happiness. The authentic teacher will step to the side of their teachings and let the student abandon them as individuals as they engage in the teachings for themselves. Great teachers help others explore; shadow-driven teachers discourage self-exploration.

My heart breaks every time I encounter toxic teachers with good teachings. But this is not the first or last time I am likely to be disappointed or discouraged by a false teacher or an ego-driven leader. That is the reason we must continue to access our own inner teacher ourselves and set the example for others to do so.

The false teacher or leader is in pursuit of some outer achievement or experience and is driven from the outside-in. And this false teacher uses inferior means to achieve what they want, including manipulation and contrivances. They are, I am sure, caught up in their false narrative and title. I can put into one phrase what makes a false teacher false and dangerous: They do not live life from the inside out. They have not, like you, taken the walk in and down to the center of themselves confronting the dark aspects and claiming their inner light.

One of my first teachers, Colleen Brenzy, taught how to know when we are in the presence of a good teacher, a safe teacher: the energy goes both ways and you don't shrink when you are with them. You both can be big; there is room for everyone to be big. I am grateful that this valuable lesson is passed on in my work with others, as Amy, a licensed psychotherapist and spiritual guide shares:

> A little over a year ago I found out that a beloved mentor I had worked with for over seven years had given into shadow wounds that involved highly unethical behavior with clients who sought him for healing. About the time that this occurred I was beginning to doubt my abilities to help people as a therapist. In the midst of feeling a crisis of confidence with my work and confusion and hurt over the loss of my mentor I visited my mother. There I saw a book on her kitchen counter entitled: The Zero Point Agreement. For whatever reason, I knew I had to find out more about this author and teacher. On her website I read that the author, Julie Tallard Johnson, specialized in ethical behavior of teachers, therapists, and healers. Be it luck or be it divine intervention that I saw Julie's book that day, I was happy when she returned my email with a time for us to meet. During our first meeting, Julie asked what might have caused me to consider quitting being a therapist. I burst into tears, which surprised me, as it is not easy for me to cry in front of anyone. The words that came out of my mouth surprised me as well.
>
> "I feel like I'm hurting people," I said.
>
> As painful as it was to recognize that was how I felt, that moment opened the door for me to understand myself on a deeper level of truth than ever before. I realized how much I gave my power away to people I believed to have more power than myself, thus denying myself the ability to truly trust my own voice, knowledge, and experience.

I have met brilliant teachers in the past. I believe these teachers have helped people, sometimes in very significant ways. However looking back many of these teachers also placed a value on their power as teacher over the emotional safety of the student. The strange thing was I didn't experience this with my recent mentor, not consciously at least, and not until I understood things at the end. He wasn't dominating or demanding. In fact I initially found him to be amazingly disarming, genuine, and brilliant at diffusing anxiety in vulnerable seekers of truth and healing.

So how in my seven plus years of working with and studying under this mentor had I come to doubt myself so fully? He encouraged us, especially through the last year I spent with him, to "become big." I interpreted this to mean he wanted us to become as big as him. It seemed like a worthy goal, but on some level impossible, after all, I had made him out to be a giant, not totally perfect, but more powerful and influential than I could ever imagined being. Looking back I realized that although he verbally invited us to become big I noticed myself, and others under his guidance, shrinking. I began to recognize a seductive quality about his support and teachings that seemed to foster a desire for his attention and approval, as well as evidence that we were special in some way.

I observed within myself and others a need for us to prove our specialness to him and not ourselves. This fostered a competitiveness on a subtle yet noticeable level by myself and others in my teaching group I have spoken with that I believe prevented us from discovering the true nature of our own equal bigness. I take responsibility for my own choices and behaviors. My choices are mine to claim, especially now in my healing process.

The betrayal I felt upon learning of my mentor's history of harmful and unethical behavior was countered with a feeling of relief. As if some voice I had ignored all these years was finally validated. I had made my mentor the Great Oz. I understand now that ethical and conscious teachers won't encourage others to see them as "special," as he did. He always had secret formulas given to him by the Spirits who he alone appeared to have access to. He would reveal my inner workings to me, as if he had a secret passage into my very own soul, that I didn't even feel I had. He taught us how to read the inner workings of others, however, I never thought I had the power to do it as well as he did which made me feel I had less ability to help people, as if it were my job to give people their meaning and understanding of themselves. In essence, I began to forget one of the most important values I have as a therapist: that the client is their own healer. I have come to learn that ethical teachers, or even friends for that matter, don't invade our inner realms in this way. The best teachers don't act as if they have a special access to spiritual truths, to God or the spiritual world.

Through my work with Julie I was about to find out how to believe in myself again. This was not done through any special ritual or instruction but through dialogue and her being present with me as I discovered my own truths. During one of my sessions with her, we talked about my fears of claiming my personal power and the mixed messages I received from my previous mentor. Julie looked at me with the most serious and intense gaze and said: "Amy, you are the biggest person in this room. And I am the biggest person in this room. How is that true?" There are some moments in life where you can actually feel a shift occurring in your body, things rearranging as an important truth emerges. That was the second time in my life I recall witnessing such a shift. It is so big a realization that what I feel from it I don't have all the words for yet. But it is from where all my knowing of myself now begins. Julie held up an amazing mirror for me that day, teacher to teacher, and I am forever grateful.

My story continues as I participate in a circle with Julie and as I reclaim my shared bigness with everyone in this circle and beyond. I am ready to serve again, and to participate in the world as the teacher and spiritual friend I know I am.

The authentic leader, as shown throughout this book, places his or her attention on their own motivations and behaviors and how these might influence others. They are guided by that internal compass of integrity and have individual ways to follow this inner teacher in the most challenging of situations. Parker shared with me on several occasions as he helped reveal my treasures as a leader: "Authentic leaders in all settings—from families to nation-states—aim at liberating the heart, their own and others', so that the heart's powers can liberate the world."

A PARADOX OF LEADERSHIP

Theseus wasn't obligated to marry Ariadne because she gifted him the red thread. None of us should feel obligated to others in this way or in any way, ever. Yet. We are responsible to and for everything that crosses our path. We are responsible in our responses. We are responsible now to pass on the red thread. How we respond to our situations, as I have already pointed out, is how we lead. The greatest paradox of leadership for me is that we are responsible to others in big ways and that this responsibility takes several forms of letting go.

My September walks take a bit longer although I go the same distance. This is because I take the time to pick up the caterpillars that are on this country road. I pick them up because from my larger view I can see that they are likely not to make it across alive. I have proof of this because there is always a collection of dead caterpillars along my way. I pick them up, say a prayer on them and place them in the grass in the same direction they were headed. Some look dead but are actually basking in the comfort of the warm sun. I apologize to them for disrupting their comfort and place them into the tall grass too.

Now, is this good leadership or just a flavor of my co-dependency? This is an expression of my leadership. I am only moving them out of harm's way, then letting them go. Also, I do not vex over those who have gotten run over; there is nothing I could have done for them. I will continue to pick up those friends in the road, walking or basking, to then let them go, let them be.

Do I stop when I am driving my car along roads where there are caterpillars? No. This would endanger me and other drivers.

And, this is a profound loss of the big picture. There are so many paradoxes in our leadings, some of which you may discover and explore along your own walks.

Trussed

It is not we who are to be tested in the trials that await,
but those principles on which we stand.
In this knowing should be comfort
and peace.

Blind in a way are all our travels and trusting.

Don't try to keep your heart from breaking.
That is as it should be.
But trust the mettle of love more than anything else
as your beam, and when you fall, fall
full-knowing into the soft folds of compassion.
Even those you can't see.

CHAPTER TEN

KEEPING HOLD OF THE RED THREAD IN THE WORLD: THE CLAIM TO AUTHENTIC SELFHOOD

What we see is simple but often ignored: the movements that transform us, our relations, and our world emerge from the lives of people who decide to care for their authentic selfhood. They decide no longer to act on the outside in a way that contradicts some truth about themselves that they hold deeply inside. They decide to claim authentic selfhood and act it out—and their decisions ripple out to transform the society in which they live, serving the selfhood of millions of others.

—Parker J. Palmer

"They" in the above quote refers to the Nelson Mandelas and the Rosa Parkses of the world. But "they" also refers to those of us who decide not "to act on the outside in a way that contradicts some truth" within ourselves. You. Me. Those of us who are willing and ready to be our "full self in the world"—this means everywhere, in all our roles and relationships. *Keeping hold of the red thread means to listen to inner truth, follow our heart, and agree not to live divided or secret lives. And I believe we will "serve the selfhood of millions," today and in the future, far beyond our gaze as we do.*

There is a lot more to Theseus's story and life after he leaves

Adriadne on the shore. There are also more stories to Ariadne's life. So both the student and teacher in us move out beyond this metaphorical labyrinth and into our daily relationships and vocational lives. And that is where, hopefully, we make certain that we keep hold of the red thread and in contact with our true nature, in all settings and roles.

When we keep hold of the red thread, we feel our belonging even during times of greatest difficulty. We are in contact with our inner knowings and our principles. We are always walking the **Inner Labyrinth**. While we have hold of the red thread, relationships are experienced as reciprocal and there is a tangible mutuality; we are moving forward in our life while taking one day at a time. Even in our aloneness we are not alone because we can experience our solitude with a belonging to self and to others who also have hold of their red thread. For me, when we have hold of the red thread, there is a bounty of meaningful coincidences because we are engaged in the eternal conversation with our spiritual source and true self.

We know we have lost hold of our red thread when our life (or a part of our life) feels as if it is not our own, when we are the effect rather than the cause of our life. We have lost the red thread of our belonging and are in a place that is more about survival than living.

When we are caught up in our fear, resentment, doubt, isolation, or other negative states, we need to find our red thread. If we are feeling empty in an area of our life, we likely have left the red thread at the door and entered a secret life, next to the soulful life. You may find yourself feeling divided, living a false or hidden life alongside the more authentic one. Such a contradiction this discovery can be! We are whole but not so in every role of our life.

> **Almost there? Birds forage farther
> into the woods of late, abandoning survival handouts.
> A March snow has them back at the feeders,
> heaps new cold on my frozen doubt too—packed hard
> in the deep, with another *I knew it*.
> I know some things else too. The birds
> are not bound to the feeder.
> And one day this belly will thaw.**

OUR SECRET LIVES

Writing is a true vocation for me. A benefit of being a writer is that I find clues to my own truth in my writing. My inner callings speak to me through the stories and poetry I write as well as from those stories and poems I receive from other authors and poets. The danger comes in not listening to my own writings for the clues they hold. The danger comes in forgetting that the stories passed on to and through me are still mine to learn from. The danger comes when I keep some personal truth cognitive or trapped on the page and begin to live a secret life.

I have written much about living a life of possibility, of knowing that there is so much more available to us than what we see with our personal limited views—views that are based on our assumptions, projections, and fears. I have written and am still writing about how to open our view to see what is truly possible. What happens when we don't see for ourselves what is possible and as a result live a secret life? We trip up. We fall off the edge of our familiar path.

Or, we may be walking along some well-worn path, in some well-known role, not harming anyone, but are not fully awake to what is beneath our feet. So we trip. We fall. We find ourselves in a precarious situation. We become depressed or anxious. We are surprised because this path was so well-worn by many good people before us. And it is a familiar path, one we know how to walk. At the late stage of turning sixty, I found I was relying on a well-worn path and role that was no longer true for me. The particular role I was in is not important. It can be any role we find ourselves in: a role within family, friendship, marriage, occupation, or community.

I was given the following story when I was eight years old and I used it in the opening of my most recent book, *The Zero Point Agreement*.

> There was a monk who appreciated his walks along a cliff that overlooked the vast ocean. This path was well used and worn. One day, perhaps not noticing that there was some erosion, or he just wasn't paying attention, he slipped and fell. As he fell over the edge of the cliff, he grabbed onto a small branch of a tree that hung out from the cliff. After catching his breath and maintaining a good

grip on the branch, he looked up. He was close enough to maneuver his way back up. But peeking over the edge was a tiger hungrily looking down at him. He looked beneath him. There was no way to climb down. Letting go of the branch would mean a certain fall to his death. He looked around for other options and saw a beautiful strawberry growing alone on a cliff vine within reach. Oh, how beautiful and sweet it looked to him! But he would surely fall if he were to grab it.

He glanced up again to see the tiger waiting patiently. He looked below at his fall. He waited. Nothing changed. The ocean was shimmering, so vast.

He sighed, took a breath, reached for the strawberry, and enjoyed it as he let go of the branch.

I thought of myself as living like this monk—taking hold of opportunity, taking risks, and trusting there would always be other possibilities within my reach. I was living like this. But as it turned out, not entirely. I had walked certain paths too many times and had gotten into the habit of not watching where I was putting my feet.

Marriages, friendships, jobs—all the roles we hold in life—can become like a secret room we enter if we don't maintain an honest and consistent consciousness with ourselves in all areas of our life. We can easily find ourselves in roles or relationships where, for a myriad of reasons, we leave our true self at the door. It could be we are focused on keeping our jobs or homes. It could be we believe we are doing the "right" thing by staying put. We might feel financially bound to a job or a primary relationship. We might come to believe that it "only takes one to save a marriage." We may be "doing it for the kids." Perhaps we can't give up a job or relationship that we felt destined to be in from the start. It could be we have become habitual and unconscious in this particular area of our life out of fear of the unknown. We may be in denial—a trait most of us learn early in life. We may have learned that living a divided life is an acceptable norm. There are too many stories of spiritual teachers, for example who are great at teaching yoga or shamanism but live a divided life through their sexual misconduct.

I first heard this story of the monk and the strawberry from a progressive Lutheran minister who later left the ministry to pursue other dreams. I recognize this young minister as one of my teachers. This story has resurfaced, and I recently had an experience wherein I found myself on that cliff. The tiger sat on the edge above me, hungrily looking down. One option was to hang out there and wait to see if someone would come along and rescue me. I knew how to do that—stay and wait.

Beyond the tiger is a well-worn path, so somebody might come by, scare the tiger away, and help me up. The rescuer will have his or her own story around his or her rescuing. Once rescued, you are now caught up in their story.

There are other directions the story can take. The branch may break. The tiger may finally give up and go away. But being on the cliff, having already relied on that worn path, metaphorically means that we likely have been there a long time, and someone else who trusts that old path (our rescuer) may end up down there with us. (Now we have two people and only one strawberry!) I want to caution you about waiting to be rescued by circumstances. If we let circumstances rescue us, we remain the effect rather than the cause of our future life.

A paradox in this story is that all choices result in death. Well, welcome to our one universally shared experience and the end to everyone's story: we die. We lose everything. At some point we will be separated from everything we love and cherish. Knowing this, what choice would be most meaningful? What choice would bring more wholeness to our life?

Knowing loss is inevitable, what do we choose? Eat the strawberry, wait to be rescued by circumstance (meaning spend more time hanging out there on the cliff, enjoying the view of the ocean), fall, or be eaten by the tiger?

> *So many things are possible just so long as you don't know they're impossible.*
>
> —Norton Juster, *Phantom Tollbooth*

REACHING FOR THE STRAWBERRY

The story of the monk hanging from the cliff is a metaphorical tool to help us feel what it's like to risk or not to risk everything for that strawberry—that immeasurable, unknown possibility. The story teaches us that we have to be able to let go of everything to make what is possible, possible. This is what happens when our true self reveals to us that we are living some form of secret life.

I went for the strawberry. I let go of the branch of a particular familiar pattern, which had a lot to do with me isolating myself and dividing one area of my life from another.

When we let go, we can't know what will happen. What won't happen is we won't remain stranded on some cliff hanging on for dear life thinking the view of the ocean is enough to sustain us. We won't place our happiness on what someone else does or doesn't do. We won't sacrifice our self on the altar of someone else's fears or perceptions. Keeping the house, the job, or our image won't be as important as making more room for our soul, our life. This letting go always includes a letting go of something or some way of life we identified with.

Our main vocation in life, as it turns out, is to be. Be whole. Be who we already are.

So this is what it can mean to let go of the branch as we keep hold of the red thread: *We face into the unknown and live in the present uncertainty as we let go of what's safe and familiar. We face gently into what we resist. We take 100 percent responsibility for our experiences and do not blame others or outer circumstances for our choices. We don't blame our bosses, spouses, or finances. We consciously live from the inside out, from the Zero Point agreement of living life from your side. We do our best to trust the ability of others to navigate their own lives even when our risk-taking may impact them. We consider and respect others as we let go, because everything we do touches everyone else.* I hadn't any clear idea of what my fall would be like or where and how I would land.

A friend shared this with me: "God is not limited by our lack of imagination." In other words, the possibilities are beyond our present imaginings.

When I was young and living at home I had two repetitive dreams. In one of the dreams, my home was either a Nazi concentration camp or "hell," with the head of the place being someone utterly evil. I would find a way to escape. Then, realizing I had left my younger sister there, I would go back to rescue her. Sometimes I succeeded; sometimes I was captured and imprisoned again. In the second dream, a white horse, free of a saddle and reins, would arrive below my upstairs bedroom window. It waited there for me to jump out, land safely on her back, and ride away.

The first dream points to my inner knowings of my traumatic surroundings and also suggests my desire and ability to escape. I was capable of saving myself, but my love for my sister called me back. The second dream, which I knew intuitively then and consciously later, represented my true self. Once on the horse, I would be living my true life, following my true callings.

On one of my morning walks while writing this chapter, I saw a small goat in a neighbor's yard. I have always wanted a goat!

"Hello!" I said.

A young woman, probably in her early twenties, said, "Hi."

"Is this a pet?" I asked.

"Yes." Her mother then joined us, and I met her for the first time, though I had been passing her house for years. She shared how her daughter also had a large sheep that thought her daughter was her mother. The young woman beamed.

"So are you involved in an animal-related vocation?" I asked the young woman.

"I wish," she said. I saw the stress of this wish flash across her face as she explained, "I'm in nursing."

I petted the goat and said my good-byes.

I wondered on my return home: *What prevents this woman from pursuing the vocation of her dreams?* She had hinted, too, that nursing wasn't necessarily her chosen profession. So what was she doing investing her money, education, and soul in it? Would not having pursued her dream vocation create a divided life for her? Would she find herself on a cliff someday, reaching out for what was possible for her? Would she be resentful toward someone or circumstances of her life if she found herself unhappy in her chosen vocation of nursing?

FACING INTO OUR RESISTANCE

What is it you resist? Where do you feel divided? When I was on the cliff, I found myself resisting authority and trying to make others the source of my problem. In this, I resisted outside help. (*I can help myself, thank you very much!* I thought). I also resisted being vulnerable, and I worried that I would be seen as a fool.

So begin exploring resistance by noticing where your resistance comes up. Then gently face into it. If you resist joining in; can you explore joining in? If you resist speaking up, can you face into this and notice where and with whom it comes up?

After letting go of the branch (that was likely about to break anyway) and reaching for the strawberry I landed in Al-Anon. I told myself I'd go to six meetings to check it out. In the past, to say I resisted Al-Anon and the 12-steps was an understatement. I felt I was above them. After all, I have been facilitating circles for decades. How could a group of nonprofessionals help me?! (How's that for resistance and arrogance? I felt a bit like Dorothy in *The Wizard of Oz*—there is nothing in the wizard's box for me here!) Turns out I found community and wisdom right from the start of my first meeting and still do today.

We can use our resistance as a nudge to turn *toward* rather than *away from*, to stop pounding on a closed door behind us and face what is moving toward us. What we must have in order to face gently into what we resist is vulnerability.

We can also change our mind. We can break a promise, let go of what *is* for what is about to be. As mentioned above, a lived life is full of broken promises. Someone or some opportunity may indeed come into our life, and we can see destiny's play at hand. But what this means is not a fixed thing. Our departures, broken promises, and break-ups are part of any relationship's narrative and destiny.

> I wonder
> how no one noticed her
> noticing so much.
> As if the rabbit-eared girl she dug out of the hill
> wasn't such a big deal. Nor the Lumbs, watching on,
> amused. Now perhaps
> her hopes are smaller these days. She could paint
> you another picture, or
> maybe you might still find the trail of wonder
> if she points out her new purple rug.

FACING INTO IT ALL

It was the end of my second Al-Anon meeting, and they chose to close by holding hands and saying the Lord's Prayer. Here was my opportunity to develop my exit strategy. What's with this Our Father "stuff"? I wondered. What had happened to the more user-friendly Serenity Prayer? Was this just more religious dogma disguised as a helpful peace offering? I was crossing rushing waters, and the last thing I needed was believing "Thy will be done." How could this place be hospitable to my Buddhist practice? Two things kept me facing into the experience: first, I had agreed to attend at least six Al-Anon meetings before I decided whether or not to continue; and second, I felt my inner pattern and dynamic of **either-or**-ing kicking in.

So I asked myself: *Where is the **both-and**?* I let myself host this edge of resistance and remembered that my first teacher, after all, had been a Lutheran minister, and that I too had this prayer memorized by heart. I brought to mind the Three R's and asked: *What is this truly about?* I considered the Buddhist mantras I chant and how the Lord's Prayer could be experienced in a similar way.

When I got home I searched for the book by Neil Douglas-Klotz, *Prayers of the Cosmos: Meditations on the Aramaic Words of Jesus*. The entire book is a unique translation and commentary on the Lord's Prayer. He takes each stanza of the prayer and gives us another, longer interpretation of its meaning. He points to a **both-and** where, no matter what your religious affiliation, you can appreciate your own meaning of its message. Douglas-Klotz also points to the value of how words sound—much like Buddhist chants—as they are said out loud: "Like other ancient native languages around the planet, Aramaic is rich in sound-meaning." In his introduction, Douglas-Klotz invites us to explore the prayer in our own way: "A tradition of both native Middle Eastern and Hebraic mysticism says that each statement of sacred teaching must be examined from at least three points of view: the intellectual, the metaphorical, and the universal (or mystical)."

The King James version of line five of the Lord's Prayer is as follows: Give us this day our daily bread, *Hawvlan lachma d'sunquanan yaomana* in Aramaic. Or this translation by Neil Douglas-Klotz: "Grant what we need each day in bread and insight."

I am so grateful for the red thread teachings of facing into experiences with hospitality, curiosity, and fearlessness. This teaching of facing into life's encounters with a curiosity afforded me freedom to explore further. Had I turned away I would not have discovered Al-Anon as a place for part of my continued journey and belonging. I would have missed this opportunity to be friends with this part of me that wants to separate and divide.

BOTH-AND: GOOD-BYE AND HELLO

During those times when we feel we have lost our hold on the red thread, we can trust that the clues are always here. We can explore what is in front of us now. We can return to the teachings that sustain us.

When difficulty arises "out there," we can reflect inwardly as the Confucian philosopher Mencius encourages us to do:

If one loves others, and they do not respond in the same way, one should turn inward and examine one's own love.
If one greets others politely, and they do not return politeness, one should turn inward and examine one's own politeness.
When one does not realize what one desires, one must turn inward and examine oneself in every point.

I leave you now, Dear Reader. Part of me wants to keep writing this book, but it's time again to head out and to trust. Trust that my writings and shared experiences have served you somehow. Trust my abilities and capacities to continue to receive the lessons that I need to learn from the red thread teachings of my life.

As I leave you In this time of social distancing, injustice and division, I see how we are all on a cliff together with a tiger above and a deathly fall below. We must face our Minotaurs, take that real step out beyond our own lives, and do what needs to be done. We must become the Theseuses and Ariadnes of our time no matter what the outcome of a single event, be it an election or natural disaster. Theseus's time in history was considered a major cultural threshold. We are at such a threshold. If each of us, or enough of us, reach for possibility and risk losing the familiar for the unknown, we may actually save our environment and democracy one heroic step at a time within our day-to-day lives. We may, if we pause to look, see that we each hold the red thread of lifetimes of teachings and wisdom that we can pass on to one another. Right here. Right now.

Let go. Pass it on.

The Red Thread

A mad mystic, a beautiful witch with thunder in her bones
Lightening from her heart lights up the window behind her
Illuminated in light and shadow as they dance inside her
The red thread in her hand sparkles for a second then goes dark
I drive 2 hours in a thunderstorm, flooding and thunder that rattle my core
Wake up child, see the light, remember

Arriving home, I know I am on the cusp of a grand threshold
I draw back into myself to a horizon I cannot yet see
I spend a year with 6 glorious people, broken and whole all at once
I find a part of myself long lost to me in the art of inwardness
She hid herself in the dark, tender space around my heart, weeping and praying to be seen
My tribe awakened my fullness, a becoming through unbecoming
Spirit rose up within me, illuminating my darkest crevices
I turned sideways and caught a glimpse of a powerful
beauty in the mirror
With a red thread in her hand

—Kimberly Lempart

A MESSAGE FROM PARKER J. PALMER

FROM TEACHER TO TEACHER: OUR RED THREAD LINEAGE

by Parker J. Palmer

I was blessed with a long line of mentors. Writing about all of them in detail would require an appendix longer than this book. So, now that I've spent eighty years following a thread that was woven, in part, from who my mentors were and what they taught me, I'll write about those who appeared early in my life.

My first mentor was my father, Max J. Palmer. Dad grew up in a blue-collar family in Waterloo, Iowa. When he graduated from high school, he went to Chicago during the Great Depression, took a temporary bookkeeping job with a company, and over the course of sixty years, became that company's CEO and owner.

On the surface, his business was selling china and silverware to commercial dining establishments. But deeper down, his real business was growing the people who worked for him through a rare combination of unconditional regard and high expectancy. He created a force field around his employees that conveyed two messages: "I believe in you" and "I am confident that you can learn and grow."

As his son, I grew up in that same force field. In my case, Dad offered unconditional love: I knew that nothing I could do would cause him to stop loving me, ever. The expectancy with which he surrounded me—which wasn't tied to specific "expectations"—was an open invitation to follow my own path and take all sorts of risks that weren't common for boys coming of age in the conformist 1950s.

The combination was critical. Risk-taking is crucial to growth, but it always comes with a chance of failure, and since failure may mean losing the respect of pivotal people in one's life, why take risks? But when a boy has unconditional love from his father, he will take the risks that growing requires, knowing that if he falls, he will not lose the love that will help him get back up and carry on. I've done the best I know how to pass along the gift my father gave me to others in my life, both in personal relationships and in programmatic expressions. For example, the retreat work done by the Center for Courage & Renewal is shaped by this combination of unconditional regard and expectancy.

In 1957 I entered Carleton College in Northfield, Minnesota. As a first-generation college student, I felt intimidated by Carleton's intellectual culture. I'm sure I would have dropped out had I not met three of the most influential mentors of my life: David Maitland, chaplain and professor of religion; Bardwell Smith, professor of religion and Asian studies; and Ian Barbour, professor of religion (who also held a PhD in physics from the University of Chicago).

These men were well known to many in the academic community for their remarkable careers as teachers, writers, and public intellectuals. To me they are important for personal reasons. Each in his own way gave me a gift that great mentors almost always give their apprentices: they saw more in me than I saw in myself. Equally important, they "put wheels" on my potentials by offering me opportunities to partner with them in various projects, including academic research. Their mentoring went well beyond affirmation: they created working situations where I could develop the habits required for good work in any field, including academics.

This trio of mentors gave me another gift I've treasured for many years, ever since I came to understand its value. In all three of them, faith and reason, religion and science cohabited in harmony. When I began my graduate work at the University of California, Berkeley, I was struck by the number of intellectuals who were actively engaged in the "war between religion and science," as if the only things that matter in trying to understand the world are things that can be weighed and measured. No wonder their view of the world was so one-dimensional, so externalized, so deficient in its grasp of the subjective dimension that human beings bring to everything they feel, believe, think, and do.

Breaking out of this limited worldview eventually became a lifelong agenda for me. Much of my work has been about the "dance" of the inner and outer lives in realms ranging from personal growth to education to social change. But long before I had the confidence to mount an intellectual case in support of the inner-outer paradox, I had a simple inward defense against the distorted worldview held by many of my professors at Berkeley. On more than a few occasions, I said to myself, *I was educated at Carleton by three people at least as smart as you are, people for whom faith and reason were not at war. So why should I swallow the party line?* My mentors silently "ran cover" for me until I gained the confidence necessary to run my own ground game.

The mentoring I received from my father and from my Carleton professors was followed by yet another set of mentors who showed up as I began getting established in my professional life. Much of the work I wanted to do could not be done inside institutions, so I had to develop the capacity to develop independent work. Step one is having a good idea that meets some significant need and learning how to articulate it in a compelling way as a fundable project. Step two is looking for start-up money, which, in my case, meant learning how to work with philanthropic foundations.

I soon learned that the best foundation officers are not mere clerks who write checks. If what you propose to do makes sense to them, they become active partners in helping you to shape, execute, and evaluate your project. They are, in fact, the best partners one can have because the nature of their work keeps them in touch with kindred people and projects around the world, giving people like me access to information that would otherwise be hard to come by.

One such mentor was Robert W. Lynn at the Lilly Endowment. I was working on a project regarding the church's involvement in public life, which has long been seen as problematic in many parts of the Christian community. For ten months running, Bob invited me to spend a day at the Endowment's offices, sometimes in conversation with him, sometimes with a group of clergy from Indianapolis where the Lilly Endowment is located. Between meetings, he asked me to prepare a "white paper" on what I had learned at the last meeting, and that paper became the springboard for the next meeting.

At the tenth meeting, where we spent some time assessing where we were in conceptualizing this project, Bob said something that caught me off guard: "We've talked about this for ten months now, and you've generated a stack of papers with a lot of actionable ideas. So when are you going to write the book?" Surprised by the question, I said I didn't know; in fact, I didn't know that a book was part of the plan. Bob said, "There's no better way than a book to maximize the chance that these ideas will get planted and start growing. So until you're ready to write it, we're done talking about it. It's time to fish or cut bait."

To make a long story short, *The Company of Strangers: Christians and the Renewal of America's Public Life* was published in 1983, and functioned exactly as Bob said it would, turning an interesting conversation into a seedbed of ideas that churches across the country began working with. At exactly the time I needed it, I was blessed with a mentor who pushed me out of the nest into the world of action.

From that moment onward, I was committed to "putting wheels on ideas" as often as I could, creating vehicles that people could ride toward real destinations in the real world, moving from mere words to "the word made flesh"—a vital part of my "red thread lineage." I can't imagine having taken that step without the encouragement of a wise mentor who was part of my "red thread" lineage.

Soon these framed spaces will be empty of us,
and us empty as turned-out pockets. Lightened,
(we trust)
in unpredictable ways.

What do I tell the one who waits now on the step,
and the ones who turn up at dusk,
trusting?
Something about starting over. Trust,
going forward will be up to you.

ENDNOTES

THE LABYRINTH, AND THE CLUE OF THE RED THREAD

1. Geiger, H. "Theseus In the Labyrinth," MANAS Reprint, Vol. 4 (1964).

2. Geiger, H. "Theseus In the Labyrinth."

CHAPTER ONE: TAKING HOLD OF THE RED THREAD: LIVING LIFE FROM THE INSIDE OUT

3. The Zero Point Agreement is "I live life from my side." Read more in Julie Tallard Johnson's book *The Zero Point Agreement: How to Be Who You Already Are* (Destiny Books, 2013).

4. An excellent reference for studying emotional dynamics is *Letting Go: The Pathway of Surrender* by David R. Hawkins (Veritas Publishing, 2012).

5. Witnesses say the facilitator, a self-proclaimed guru, encouraged people who were passing out, hallucinating, and vomiting—symptoms of extreme heat stroke—to fight the discomfort and stay in the lodge as long as possible. Those seeking a true spiritual awakening, he told them, needed "to surrender to death to survive it." [Various sources, including Bloomberg.com]

6. Five Habits of the Heart may be found in Parker J. Palmer's book *Healing the Heart of Democracy: The Courage to Create a Politics Worthy of the Human Spirit* (Jossey-Bass, 2011).

CHAPTER TWO: UNWINDING THE THREAD: LIVING WITH CONTRADICTIONS

7. For several years, The Power of And was the motto of the University

of Wisconsin, Eau Claire. It signaled the fact that they encouraged students to explore more than one path of study and vocation.

8. Parker J. Palmer frequently discusses the notion of paradox, and this line comes from the prologue to Thomas Merton's book *The Sign of Jonas*. Parker was deeply influenced by Merton's writings.

CHAPTER NINE: HANDING OTHERS THE RED THREAD: LEADERSHIP AS EVERYONE'S VOCATION

9. For those readers who teach within the educational system, Parker J. Palmer's book, *The Courage to Teach,* is a must read.

10. For more on hosting others' edges, please read Parker's book, *A Hidden Wholeness,* especially his discussion on how to facilitate circles of trust. No matter how you lead others, I recommend that you explore Parker's teachings on circles of trust and skilled leadership. He also offers his teachings through the nonprofit Center for Courage and Renewal, which offers workshops and training on the courage to teach and lead. <www.couragerenewal.org>

BIBLIOGRAPHY

Arterburn, Stephen, and Jack Felton. *Toxic Faith: Experiencing Healing from Painful Spiritual Abuse.* Colorado Springs, Colo.: Waterbrook Press, 2001.

Bohm, David, and F. David Peat. *Science, Order, and Creativity: A Dramatic New Look at the Creative Roots of Science and Life.* New York: Bantam Books, 1987.

Bolen, Jean Shinoda. *The Tao of Psychology: Synchronicity and the Self.* 25th ed. San Francisco: HarperSanFrancisco, 2005.

Campbell, Joseph. *The Power of Myth.* With Bill Moyers. New York: Doubleday, 1988.

———. *A Joseph Campbell Companion: Reflections on the Art of Living.* Edited by Diane K. Osbon. New York: HarperCollins, 1991.

Douglas-Klotz, Neil. *Prayers of the Cosmos: Meditations on the Aramaic Words of Jesus.* New York: HarperCollins, 1990.

Ehrlich, Gretel. *A Match to the Heart: One Woman's Story of Being Struck by Lightning.* New York: Penguin Books, 1995.

———. *The Solace of Open Spaces.* New York: Penguin Books, 1985.

Emerson, Ralph Waldo. *The Essays of Ralph Waldo Emerson.* Cambridge, Mass.: Belknap Press of Harvard University Press, 1987.

———. *Self-Reliance and Other Essays.* Mineola, N.Y.: Dover Publications, 1993.

Fincher, Susanne F. *Coloring Mandalas: For Insight, Healing, and Self-Expression.* Boston: Shambhala, 2000.

Hanh, Thich Nhat. *The Heart of Understanding: Commentaries on the Prajnaparamita Heart Sutra.* Berkeley, Calif.: Parallax Press, 1988.

Johnson, Julie Tallard. *The Zero Point Agreement: How to Be Who You Already Are.* Inner Traditions/Bear & Company. Kindle Edition.

Kain, John. *A Rare and Precious Thing: The Possibilities and Pitfalls of Working with a Spiritual Teacher.* New York: Random House, 2006.

Macy, Joanna. *Mutual Causality in Buddhism and General Systems Theory: The Dharma of Natural Systems.* Albany: State University of New York Press, 1991.

Mails, Thomas E. Fools *Crow: Wisdom and Power.* Tulsa, Okla.: Council Oak Books, 1991.

Masterson, James F. *The Search for the Real Self: Unmasking the Personality Disorders of Our Age.* New York: Free Press, 1988.

McKnight, John. *The Abundant Community: Awakening the Power of Family and Neighborhoods.* Berrett-Koehler Publishers, 2012.

Miller, Alice. *The Drama of the Gifted Child: The Search for the True Self.* Rev. ed. New York: Basic Books, 1997.

Mohatt, Gerald, and Joseph Eagle Elk. *The Price of a Gift: A Lakota Healer's Story.* Lincoln: University of Nebraska Press, 2000.

Reps, Paul, and Nyogen Senzaki. *Zen Flesh, Zen Bones: A Collection of Zen and Pre-Zen Writings.* Boston: Tuttle Publishing, 1985.

Sanchez, Victor. *The Teachings of Don Carlos: Practical Applications of the Works of Carlos Castaneda.* Rochester, Vt.: Bear & Company, 1995.

———. *The Toltec Path of Recapitulation: Healing Your Past to Free Your Soul.* Rochester, Vt.: Bear & Company, 2001.

Sanford, John A. *The Kingdom Within: The Inner Meaning of Jesus' Sayings.* New York: Paulist Press, 1970.

Tzu, Lao. *Tao Te Ching*. Translated by Stephen Mitchell. New York: Harper Perennial, 1991.

Whyte, David. *The House of Belonging: Poems*. Langley, Wash.: Many Rivers Press, 1997.

———. *Pilgrim: Poems*. Langley, Wash.: Many Rivers Press, 2012.

———. *What to Remember When Waking: The Disciplines of Everyday Life*. Audio CD. Louisville, Colo.: Sounds True, 2010.

OTHER BOOKS BY JULIE TALLARD JOHNSON

Johnson, Julie Tallard. *Wheel of Initiation: Practices for Releasing Your Inner Light*. Inner Traditions/Bear & Company. 2010.

———. *Spiritual Journaling: Writing Your Way to Independence*. Inner Traditions/Bear & Company February 23, 2006.

———. *The Thundering Years: Rituals and Sacred Wisdom for Teens*. Bindu Books, April 1, 2001.

BOOKS BY PARKER J. PALMER

Palmer, Parker J. *The Active Life: A Spirituality of Work, Creativity, and Caring*. San Francisco: Harper and Row, 1990.

———. *Healing the Heart of Democracy: The Courage to Create a Politics Worthy of the Human Spirit*. San Francisco: Jossey-Bass, 2011.

———. *A Hidden Wholeness: The Journey Toward an Undivided Life*. San Francisco: Jossey-Bass, 2004.

———. *Let Your Life Speak: Listening for the Voice of Vocation*, 1st ed. Jossey-Bass, 1999.

———. *On the Brink of Everything: Grace, Gravity, and Getting Old*. Berrett-Koehler Publishers, 2018.

IN GRATITUDE

"Just in time" is a saying I have heard from friends in Al-Anon. This speaks to how people, events, and various spiritual and natural encounters can show up "just in time"—just in time for what we need.

All those who participated in my Red Thread Circles over the past ten years arrived just in time for each other, for me, and for themselves. The most recent circle (Kim, David, Angela, Jenny, Kimberly, Lori, Cheryl) had to show up through a live-virtual circle due to COVID. I am deeply grateful to have participated, facilitated, and witnessed all these circles with their arrivals and departures.

So much gratitude to my business partner with whom I collaborate and lead retreats through our work as The Yogi & the Writer™. Molly Chanson's compassionate determination to be present for herself and others gifts me every day. Her arrival in this year of "collaboration" was perfectly timed.

To all the poets and storytellers in my life! Your words and wisdom always arrive just in time, especially Rebecca Cecchini (this book's poet), Mokasiya (Alan Christensen), Kimberly Lampert, David Whyte, Carl Sandburg, William Stafford, Maya Angelou, Mary Oliver, Joy Harjo, and Claudia Schmidt.

All my teachers, past and present, arrived at my door, red thread in hand, and always in time gave me perspective, guidance, and hope: Parker J. Palmer, His Holiness the Dalai Lama, Colleen Brezny, santikaro bhikkhu, Carole Kretschman, my entire Al-Anon family, David Hawkins, David Bohm, the Sage of the *I Ching,* and the Kadampa teachers of the Lojong Teachings. And to my spiritual friend, Liz Wosniak, whose love and insights have been a light through dark times.

Christine Cote from Shanti Arts showed up to publish this book. Her keen and compassionate eye helped bring this book to its best. Anne Dillon and Cami Cenek helped with edits and reads. Erik Frydenlund, you who continue to show up in time as my manifestation and writing partner.

Always so much gratitude to my daughter, Lydia, in all her arrivals and departures as she adventures inward and out on the great adventure of her life. Her first arrival was also "just in time."

Each walk I take through Stewart Park or some other wild refuge consistently brings me the arrival of companionship and teachings I can only get among the trees and breeze.

Finally, to you, my reader, arriving to this book and these teachings. I am grateful for your reaching out to take hold of this red thread. And even more so for your handing your wisdom and love to the next weary but courageous traveler.

In a circle of gratitude,
Julie

ABOUT THE AUTHOR

Julie Tallard Johnson's writing and teaching explore the timeless relationship of human beings to their natural and inner worlds, and to others. With her nearly forty years of counseling others and leading transformational circles, Julie shares her experience and wisdom in her books, blogs, and retreats, which invite us to meet our circumstances with equanimity, curiosity, and fearlessness. She has written eleven books, which include *The Zero Point Agreement*, *The Wheel of Initiation*, and *Spiritual Journaling*. She holds a master's degree in social work and is a licensed clinical social worker. Julie collaborates closely with her business partner, yoga instructor Molly Chanson, to offer inspiring retreats for all levels of yogis and writers. For Julie's retreats, online courses (her popular one: Be the Cause of Your Life), blogs, and updates, visit her website: www.julietallardjohnson.com.

Julie resides in Mount Horeb, Wisconsin with her two dogs.

ABOUT THE POET

Rebecca Cecchini is a poet and writer from Wisconsin. A longtime itinerant on winding roads and side paths and a Dominican Associate of Sinsinawa, her writing flows from a desire to recognize and honor the life of the Spirit, through which we all have our being, our connection, and our belonging. She lives in her home town of Madison, Wisconsin, with her spouse Honora, and their two bright-eyed, four-legged boys.

Shanti Arts

Nature • Art • Spirit

Please visit us online
to browse our entire book catalog,
including poetry collections and fiction,
books on travel, nature, healing, art,
photography, and more.

Also take a look at our highly
regarded art and literary journal,
Still Point Arts Quarterly, which
may be downloaded for free.

www.shantiarts.com

www.ingramcontent.com/pod-product-compliance
Lightning Source LLC
Chambersburg PA
CBHW070612170426
43200CB00012B/2668